I0605171

ROBERT BRESSON

Robert Bresson

CINEMATIC STYLE AS PHILOSOPHY

Robert B. Pippin

THE UNIVERSITY OF CHICAGO PRESS
CHICAGO AND LONDON

The University of Chicago Press, Chicago 60637
The University of Chicago Press, Ltd., London
© 2026 by The University of Chicago
All rights reserved. No part of this book may be used or reproduced in any manner whatsoever without written permission, except in the case of brief quotations in critical articles and reviews. For more information, contact the University of Chicago Press, 1427 E. 60th St., Chicago, IL 60637.
Published 2026
Printed in the United States of America

35 34 33 32 31 30 29 28 27 26 1 2 3 4 5

ISBN-13: 978-0-226-84502-9 (cloth)
ISBN-13: 978-0-226-84504-3 (paper)
ISBN-13: 978-0-226-84503-6 (ebook)
DOI: https://doi.org/10.7208/chicago/9780226845036.001.0001

Library of Congress Cataloging-in-Publication Data

Names: Pippin, Robert B., 1948–author.
Title: Robert Bresson : cinematic style as philosophy / Robert B. Pippin.
Description: Chicago : The University of Chicago Press, 2026. | Includes bibliographical references and index.
Identifiers: LCCN 2025020663 | ISBN 9780226845029 (cloth) | ISBN 9780226845043 (paperback) | ISBN 9780226845036 (ebook)
Subjects: LCSH: Bresson, Robert. | Motion picture producers and directors—France.
Classification: LCC PN1998.3.B755 P574 2026
LC record available at https://lccn.loc.gov/2025020663

♾ This paper meets the requirements of ANSI/NISO Z39.48–1992 (Permanence of Paper).

Authorized Representative for EU General Product Safety Regulation (GPSR) queries: **Easy Access System Europe**—Mustamäe tee 50, 10621 Tallinn, Estonia, gpsr.requests@easproject.com
Any other queries: https://press.uchicago.edu/press/contact.html

Contents

1
Truth in Cinema

In Robert Bresson's breakthrough film, *Diary of a Country Priest* (1951), a very young priest arrives at his first parish. He is from the start greeted by suspicion, indifference, resentment, and hostility. School children mock him; his mentor, a neighboring priest, clearly does not think he is up to the job. The priest has no idea why there should be this sort of rudeness and coldness, and it is even more difficult for the viewer to understand. We learn nothing about the priest's background, family, education. He does not even have a name throughout the film. In *A Man Escaped* (1956), a French resistance prisoner is being transported to a Nazi jail with two other men in the back of a car. He finds the car door unlocked and bolts for freedom. Contrary to all cinematic expectations, the camera does not follow him, but stays trained on the two expressionless men remaining in the car, and we only hear the sounds of the man being recaptured. In *Pickpocket* (1959), a young, well-educated man suddenly decides without explanation to himself or the viewer to try his hand at pickpocketing at a local race track. He is soon arrested, but we do not see why, what evidence there might be. We just cut from the racetrack to him sitting in the car with the policemen. No one speaks. For reasons just as mysterious, he is released and his haul returned to him. Throughout the film, the camera lingers on empty stalls, open doors, and hands. In *Au hasard, Balthazar* (1966), the main character is the eponymous donkey, who suffers horribly throughout the film, and dies what is one of the saddest, most mysterious but most beautiful deaths in all of cinema. At the end of *Mouchette* (1967), a fourteen-year-old girl, without dialogue or voice-over, wraps herself in a white dress and rolls down a hill into a pool of water, drowning herself. In *L'Argent* (1983), a man we have come to know as a hardworking family man, after being imprisoned, is released and without visible signs of rage or distress or even reason, begins murdering people, including an entire family.

This is only a brief summary of the narrative strangeness of some of Bresson's films, but there are many more features that set his films apart from commercial movies. Actors are directed not to act, music is used very little and finally not at all, there are large ellipses in the narration, the framing of shots is unconventional and surprising. What accounts for these peculiarities?

Bresson tried to explain his approach several times, in interviews and most extensively in a small book published in 1975, *Notes on the Cinematograph*. He tells us that the thirteen filmed fictional narratives he made over a forty-year career are not even movies or "cinema" at all, and so do not invite conventional movie expectations.[1] They are, instead, "cinematographs." He insists on this because he is dissatisfied with the fact that movies have failed to make full use of the medium-specific capacities of moving photography and sound recording and have instead been content with being "filmed theater."[2] His contention is that such a compromise with theatrical conventions has resulted in aesthetic representations that are themselves theatrical, or must inevitably be experienced as staged, not credible in their presentation of a human world and so in some sense false, both untrue to what cinema can do and untrue to what should be cinema's goal: truth itself. "Truth" in what sense, with respect to what, and how achieved, are obviously immediate, unavoidable questions, and they will come up frequently in what follows. Whatever else "true" might come to

1. The bare details of Bresson's life are known, but there is as yet no personal or intellectual biography. He was classically educated in a Catholic environment, began as a painter associated with the surrealist circle, was a prisoner of war, gave many interviews throughout his life but like most artists was reluctant to talk about "the meaning" of his films. See the brief account in Cardullo (2009b), xiii. Bresson was an icon in French and international cinema for most of his career after *Diary of a Country Priest*, lionized by Godard, Truffaut, and Bazin, and greatly influential for filmmakers like Chantal Ackerman, Jean Eustache, Rainer Werner Fassbinder, Philippe Garrel, Aki Kaurismäki, Olivier Assayas, Claire Denis, Bruno Dumont, Michael Haneke, Terrence Malick, Martin Scorsese, Maurice Pialat, Atom Egoyan, and especially Jean-Pierre and Luc Dardenne, but his films have proven so demanding and art house cinemas have become so rare, that he has suffered a long period of neglect, and his name is no longer prominent among film theorists. He is now, in the words of Morris (1999), "a true anomaly even by the exacting standards of intransigent auteurs *à la* Carl Dreyer or Josef von Sternberg." See Cardullo (2009b), xii. A very useful account of something like the cult of Bresson in France, or his role in the issue of the status of the "auteur," can be found in the first chapter of Morari (2017).

2. For a discussion of various elements behind the debate about theater and film, see Morales (2023). See also Sontag (1966).

mean, it is immediately clear that it does not mean "true to life," representing life as ordinarily experienced, the province of Hollywood cinema. While it is true that in Bresson's films, people say and do things and interact in an intelligible way, and there are suicides, rapes, and murders; police shoot at robbers; people have sex; and very often, but not always, one thing leads to another as we might expect. But we don't recognize what we see as "normal" life, and it is clear that "plots" play a subsidiary role in the film's self-presentation. This, I want to show, has much to do with how Bresson regards the theatricality of daily life, its own falseness. What we immediately detect in a Bresson narrative is that much seems "subtracted" from what we normally experience, especially the (direct) expression of emotion,[3] and there are large expository gaps in the unfolding of events. For the moment, we can note that Bresson's experiment is to show that the world-on-film can be both the world-as-it-can-be-uniquely-available-to-film and yet also present various aspects of the world as such, in its truth, "how it actually is" (as opposed to how it is ordinarily experienced) in various psychological, social, and even ontological dimensions, all in ways that are uniquely available to a camera and sound recorder but not available in ordinary experience.[4] There are unquestionably Bressonian views of some great generality and scope about human existence and the problem of meaning, and what is most interesting about his work is that many of those views are intertwined with his decisions about style. This means that in order to avoid the directorial "mistake" noted above, filmed theater,[5] Bresson had to work to develop a style that has been rightly described as "austere," "rigorous," "pure," "minimalist," "bare," "essentialist," all in a way that does not distract from but enhances the primary mode of a viewer's receptivity: our "emotional" responsiveness (in a sense that needs much unpacking).

3. As Bresson intended, this paradoxically leads to a great emotional power in the films.

4. "My films are an attempt to rediscover a kind of truth, a kind of reality. I may be addicted to the real." Bresson (2013), 202. And "I am looking for truth, or the impression of truth." Robert Bresson, interview by Alain Bévérini, TF1 International, 1983.

5. There are several reasons for Bresson's distrust of theater as a model for film. (He is not criticizing theater itself, which he notes that he loves. See Bresson [2013], 192.) One is what we are now noting, that the theater, with live actors on a staged set, is reproducing life as it is ordinarily experienced, and so does not have available cinema's capacity to strip away elements of such ordinariness that obscure rather than help illuminate issues of human conflict, sociality, motivation, and sources of meaning implicit but not generally available in direct experience. But he also thinks that theater performances are largely repetitious and thus standardize performances night after night, relying largely on technique, whereas the cinema aims at an illumination that is unique, momentary, even ineffable. He also thinks that if cinema takes theater as its model, it will be taken as a mere "shadow" of live actors on a stage.

His success in this attempt would mean that we are still engaged in, deeply emotionally involved in, the world filmed, even while the film world itself looks very different from conventional cinema, and invites a different sort of absorbed attention, one inspired by a different sort of ambition. We need then to understand the distinctiveness of the cinematograph and what it could mean for such a vehicle to be the bearer of truth.[6]

Bresson tells us that he has a great deal of confidence that a camera and sound recorder can disclose something about human beings that cannot be disclosed otherwise, but only if cinema comes to realize that it needs to rewrite, as it were, the contract between artist and audience, shifting the terms from entertainment (guiding, cajoling, amusing, satisfying the audience) to the medium-specific capacities of the art. That the films are "demanding" is quite literal. They demand a kind of attentiveness unfamiliar to most movie audiences. He also thinks that traditional commercial cinema is "for the viewer," caught up in the conventions of entertainment, and he wants to insist by contrast that the viewer is there "for the film," and that this demand on the viewer is most often resisted.

The director's camera can slow events down, frame events in ways that would not show up that way normally, direct concentration on elements that go by too quickly in daily life, and so forth. Such an idea of truth as something disclosed rather than asserted is immediately controversial: most philosophers would insist that only propositions can be bearers of truth. It is the proposition that expresses whatever is disclosed that is the truth bearer. That restriction would seem extreme, though. It seems quite reasonable when someone says that she suddenly "saw" something significant about a person's character, given, say, an action that the latter just performed. If the philosopher says that what could be true in what she saw can only be the proposition that expresses *what* she saw, and that proposition could only be said to be true if we can state clearly its truth conditions and whether they have been fulfilled, then two things seem to be going wrong. First of all, it might not be possible to state determinately in propositional form just what it is she saw, even though she can be rightly convinced that the person is now disclosed not as she had thought, that is, as someone who would do *that*. And the truth conditions just take us back to the revelatory character of her experience of what she saw, and that is an interpretive issue, not an empirical one. We accept the possibility of disclosed truth as a relatively common feature of ordinary life, without accepting the strict

6. For more on the distinction between the film world and the world filmed, see the important study by Yacavone (2014). On the ontological status of film itself, or "film reality," see Rushton (2010).

determinacy and propositional restrictions. (Bresson: "One recognizes the true by its efficacy, its power." *NC*, xx.)[7]

I want to say that the first step in understanding Bresson's ambition is to understand that deliberately refusing to invite conventional cinematic absorption in a movie world is motivated by more than a commitment to aesthetic concerns, to cinematic purity, medium-specific rigorousness. It has to do with a range of radical philosophical commitments implicit in Bresson's decisions about film. I offer this as a supplement to, a different way of thinking about, what has become an understandably widespread view of the seriousness, even the solemnity, of Bresson's films: that they must reflect his views about a "transcendent" dimension of human life,[8] a religious sensibility that is honest about profound human sinfulness (even depravity) as well as its possible redemption in moments of grace, understood as a divine gift, and making possible faith. Bresson did make four films about characters who avow religious commitments, *Angels of Sin* (1943), *Diary of a Country Priest* (1951), *The Trial of Joan of Arc* (1962), and *Lancelot du Lac* (1974). Aside from that unusual focus (films about religious life and experience are relatively rare), the influence of the initial reception of *Diary of a Country Priest*, especially by Catholic critics at the *Cahiers du Cinéma*, such as André Bazin, Amédée Ayfre, Henri Agel, and Roger Leenhardt (all of whom wrote for the Catholic journal *Esprit*);[9] Susan Sontag's 1964 essay "Spiritual Style in the Films of Robert Bresson"; and the influential book by Paul Schrader, *The Transcendental Style in Film*, which appeared in 1972, helped to establish the view that Bresson was not only a religious,

7. Bresson (1986). Hereafter *NC* in the text.

8. The influential term used by Schrader (2018), one that I believe has somewhat limited the anglophone commentary on Bresson.

9. For an economical summary of the position and history of *Esprit* and the role of Bazin, see Price (2011), 7–8, and all of his introduction's summary of the religious reception of Bresson and its limitation, 1–14. This is not at all to deny that, while Bresson denies being a Jansenist or Catholic filmmaker, he is certainly willing to say such things as, when denying that his film *Mouchette* is without hope, "That's not how I see it; I believe in the soul, in God." Bresson (2013), 194. I think the most we can say is that Bresson identified as a believer, but that he is not interested in doctrinal matters, as if "being religious" were a subscription to a list of doctrines, and that he should be counted in the tradition of Republican (in the French, revolutionary sense) anticlericalism. Doctrinaire religion is another example of what he calls "ideology" and wants to avoid. In his 1976 interview with Paul Schrader, he said this in response to Schrader suggesting that he was "creating his own theology," "I see another way to answer your question. Ideology is the moral. I don't want to be ideological. I want to be true. . . . I want to make people feel life as I do: that life is life, and in everything, the most ordinary, the most material, I see ideology." Schrader (1998), 487. A Heideggerian word for such ideology would be "thoughtlessness."

but a Catholic, and even a Jansenist, filmmaker,[10] that the films are vehicles for the expression of his own religious commitments.

It should be obvious, though, that however interested Bresson was in a religious sensibility, making films about characters with religious commitments is not the same as being a "religious filmmaker," and I want to present an alternate interpretation of Bresson's enterprise. This is not to deny that many elements of his films can be interpreted in a Jansenist way, especially given Bresson's (not always positive) references to Pascal:[11] the Augustinian idea that with man's fall, our natures are irremediably corrupt, predestined, that there is no way by our own efforts or by what the Jesuits called "mental discipline," to avoid sin, and that only divine grace makes it possible to resist sin. The Jansenists take their bearings from such passages as 1 John 2:16: "For all that is in the world is the concupiscence of the flesh and the concupiscence of the eyes, and the pride of life, which is not of the Father but of this world." In the face of such inevitable depravity, the priest's final proclamation seems the only response, "All is grace."

And Bresson is clearly interested in the situation of a religious sensibility in a world where there is next to no social resonance for the expression of such commitments, especially for characters like the priest. (When asked in the Godard/Delahaye interview if he was a Jansenist, he said, "Janséniste, alors, dans le sense de dépouillement" [Jansenism, then, in the sense of austerity] [476].)[12] There is certainly a kind of religious atmosphere in some of the films, but it would be too restrictive to claim that these films mean to show us that there is only one alternative to a form of life without faith

10. For a clear account, without necessarily a commitment to the idea, of what this might mean and why viewers might feel that way, see Durgnat (1998). Cardullo (1998b) gives one of the most robust and confident views of Bresson as a "Jansenist" filmmaker, xxi and following pages. But much of what he attributes to Bresson's religiosity can stand alone as philosophical commitments, including his "distrust of psychological motives," xiv; a "time of crisis," xvi; "the total collapse of moral and ethical values in a work gone madly materialistic," xix; "a final realism that is not 'realism,'" xviii; and "the apocalyptic pessimism" of his later films, xix. My claim is that his films can also be viewed from a different perspective, one that captures more of the power of the films, not that they cannot also be viewed as evincing religious sentiments.

11. Cf. Price (2011): "Perhaps the answer is not in Pascal, as so many of Bresson's admirers often turn, but Adorno: 'The bourgeoisie wants art voluptuous and life ascetic; the reverse would be better.' 'The reverse' as Adorno puts it, is also true of Bresson," 14.

12. There is an extensive discussion of Pascal and Jansenism in Jonathan Hourigan's interview with Tim Cawkwell. Hourigan (n.d.). And it is true that Bresson said that when he made *The Trial of Joan of Arc*, "I see her with the eyes of a believer," an ambiguous claim that could as well describe his approach, what it would be to see her with the eyes of a believer, as his own faith. This is from an interview with André Parinau, cited by Leo Murray in Cameron (1969), 96.

in God, a hope for an eternal life, and grace as a divine gift enabling faith: a life of crushing despair, given the absence of faith, the primary source of that despair. Bresson is influenced by the same sensibility that one finds in Bernanos,[13] for example, although without any of the right-wing cultural politics.[14]

So, for example, we can believe that a collapse in our commitment to the world, our love of the world, is possible but that it can be restored (a kind of salvation) in a way we cannot argue ourselves into, or be argued into, that it "happens" to us much more than we effect, without believing in grace as a *divine* gift. (Although the sentiment could be called a belief in "grace" as such, but not divine.) We can believe that human life is much more characterized by egoism, exploitation, selfishness, and pure evil than we can do anything about, without that being a belief in salvation by faith alone, or we can believe in the enormous role of chance in a human life without believing in the arbitrary intervention of a deity. So one can say that there is a dimension to the films that resonates with people of faith: that, as in what the faithful believe, life cannot be an object of *intelligible* meaningfulness; that there is nothing philosophy or reason can figure out about sources of meaningfulness, no ultimate role for reason in rendering human life endurable, and that whether it is or is not endurable for us is more a matter of chance and "grace" in the above sense. Our being able to come to understand this in the right, deep way is available to us, if it is, much more probably in aesthetic experiences, especially in the films of Robert Bresson.[15]

Bresson's claim that traditional cinema mimics a falseness in our understanding of our own experiences of that world is a paradoxical notion that will take some effort to clarify, but I believe it is the key to understanding why Bresson's films can both portray the human world in filmic ways that seem so strange, unrecognizable, even sometimes inhuman, and yet claim to be disclosing something true. Hollywood cinema especially does a much better job of inviting recognition of the filmed world as what we take our experiences to be, but that portrayal, however phenomenologically right, is often a portrayal of a fantasy world. ("Filmed theater" in other words,

13. Bernanos: "the feeling of God's absence is the only sign left of his existence." Quoted by Pipolo (2010), 211.

14. I mean what is expressed in Bernanos's 1946 essay "The European Spirit and the World of Machines," in Bernanos (2019), 117–68.

15. Not to mention the fact that Bresson, who once called himself an "atheist Catholic," rejected any such ascription. (In 1974, as reported in Durgnat [1998].) "I've been called an intellectual but of course I'm not. Writing is unbelievably difficult but I have to do it, because everything must originate with me. I've been called a Jansenist which is madness, I'm the opposite." Ciment (1998), 501.

does not only refer to filming a stage play, but to filming the theatrical self-representations of daily life.)[16] There is a fragility in such a fantasy because it involves an avoidance of, or even a fleeing from, any reckoning with the nature of the historical world we actually live in. Bresson's is a dissatisfaction with a kind of ontological as well as cinematic falseness, a "false way of being in the world" as well as a parallel and related cinematic inauthenticity. Taking as "real" or realistic a presentation of the human world as "filmed theater" does indeed duplicate a possible, even prevalent human experience of that world, but one that requires strategic self-representations, self-deceit, anxious conformism, and thoughtless accommodationism, and so it is "true to life" only in reproducing the falseness of that experience.

This is not treated, at least not primarily, as a consequence of human sinfulness but is tied to the modes of being that are possible in that world, our world, the social, political, economic world that sets the horizon for possibly meaningful lives in the postwar West. Bresson's own formulations of this point are elusive, but he says enough to confirm the philosophical ambition of his enterprise.

> Not to shoot a film in order to illustrate a thesis or to display men and women confined to their external aspect. But to discover the matter they are made of. To attain that "heart of the heart" which does not let itself be caught either by poetry, or by philosophy, or by drama. (*NC*, 17)[17]

Now, in movies, even Hollywood movies, the cinematic experience of that falseness can have its own paradoxical value, one that Bresson's polemics against movies can underrate. For many movies can invite a thoughtless absorption into a mythic or fantasy world precisely in order to disclose the often dangerous power of that mythic frame or to thematize that falseness itself. Many great Westerns do the former; many great melodramas do the latter.[18] But our concern is with Bresson's attempt to avoid such irony or other forms of formal cinematic self-consciousness, all by contrast with harnessing the unique power of the camera and the microphone to disclose

16. There is no filmmaker more representative of Michael Fried's long, powerful campaign against theatricality in the arts than Bresson. See Fried (1976, 1998) and Pippin (2021a).

17. See also, "I believe what we need to rediscover in films is the automatic functions of life, as opposed to the theater, where every gesture is monitored, every word intellectually examined. For me, in my own films, gestures and words are there primarily to provoke things—or *the* thing that is the essence of the film. More so than the novel, cinematography can be a means of discovery." Bresson (2013), 147.

18. See Pippin (2010 and 2021b).

what is neglected, screened from us, thoughtlessly ignored—and this is the crucial point—in *both* ordinary cinematic absorption and in our self-understanding in the everyday world.

So just as a film can demand a different sort of engagement than is common, the human world itself can demand an out of the ordinary comportment, a struggle for a source of meaningfulness more original than what is publicly staged or commonly assumed, and these are demands that can be ignored or resisted, both in aesthetic experience and in life. My idea in the following is that Bresson's ideal of cinematic absorption, and with that the ideal of cinematic truth, is aimed at such a disclosure of the true nature of worldly absorption and existential truthfulness. Or: the sources of meaningfulness in a cinematic world, both for the characters in the filmed world and for the film world, are inseparable from the question of the general possibility of sources of meaningfulness in a historical world in general. These possibilities have become so minimal and demand such hypocrisy, conformism, and self-deceit that—as we shall see in several instances—characters live in a state of such dissatisfaction that it culminates in what Marcuse calls "The Great Refusal," and in some cases suicide.

This notion—being oriented in a world, understood as a horizon of possible meaningfulness—is not the sort of "object" that can be isolated in propositional form and asserted in judgments with clear truth conditions, to return to that earlier issue. Its contextualizing role is only available indirectly, as if out of the corner of a cinematic eye. The same inseparability is true when trying to understand the failure of meaningfulness, increasingly Bresson's interest after the mid-sixties. By meaningfulness, I mean the ways in which individuals purposively direct their lives on the basis of what has come to matter to them, and this on the assumption that something mattering, experienced as significant, is distinct from, and may even conflict with, conscious beliefs about what ought to matter, and distinct also from consciously desiring ends. Mattering in this sense is fundamental, original, primary; we "find ourselves" treating something as significant. Our engagement with anything in the world already assumes the emergence of what is salient in significance and what is negligible, and this experience does not depend on any views we might hold about what is or should be of significance. (Something can matter to us that we think ought not to matter, or we can believe something ought to matter to us but know that it actually doesn't matter, even if we take action to secure it.) This feature of human life can be especially powerfully present when it is absent, as, most acutely, in *Mouchette*, as we shall see.

We tend to think of meaningfulness as radically individual, that what might matter to one farmer in a small village need not matter to another, or to a young student in Paris. But such individual inflections of meaning are inflections of a common historical world, the shared historical world of the second half of the twentieth century. And this notion of a world, as used by Heidegger, this horizon of possible meaningfulness, is not, as noted, itself available as any sort of object *in* the world. It is available only in worldly comportments, doings, and projects, where "available" is clearly in the "can be shown but not fully and explicitly said" category. Bresson believes that it is uniquely, if also indirectly and elliptically, available to the camera and the sound recorder. The same inseparability of individual matterings and world-historical possibilities is true when trying to understand the failure of meaningfulness, the main theme of Bresson's later films, beginning with *Au hasard, Balthazar*.

The mention of any philosopher, even one as "post-philosophical" in the traditional sense as Heidegger, in any book on film (as I have found in reaction to other books of mine on what is now called "film-philosophy") immediately raises a concern that one is treating the film as a mere vehicle for ideas, or a container of philosophical claims.[19] But, first, any literary or cinematic criticism is worthless if it just tries to paraphrase what goes on in the film, or just redescribes what is particular about its formal technique, and must rather seek by some form of writing to appeal to the experience of the film to illuminate what it means that the director put together the scenes that he or she did, made the thing that way and not another. A film can be considered something like a speech-act, where understanding it is a matter not only of understanding what is said, but what the point of saying it then, in that context, is. One wants to know what it means that the priest cannot pray, even when he is dying; that a man would choose to make a film about a donkey's suffering; that a fourteen-year-old girl would commit suicide in

19. The following is a response to a version of this sort of criticism by Burnett (2017), according to whom I am treating Bresson as a "Heideggerian philosopher." That is not accurate. I realize and try to respect the fact that Bresson is a filmmaker, not a philosopher. The point that his cinematic style implies philosophical commitments commits one to an intense engagement with such style, as I hope to have done. Equally off base is the charge that "Pippin insists that Bresson wanted his movies to conjure *thoughts*." The whole point of the invocation of Heidegger is to suggest that Bresson intends an absorption in his cinematic world that is at least immediately, on first viewing, nondiscursive, an attunement to meaning that mirrors the availability of the world in the film world to characters. Particularly misplaced is the charge that what I am doing is philosophy "instead of studying the films." I hope the details of the following belie such a charge. To be fair to Burnett, he is basing his critique on one very brief article on *Au hasard, Balthazar* published in *Liberties* (Pippin [2023]). I hope the full scope of this book makes clear that I am not trying to turn Bresson into a philosopher. See also the introductory chapter to Pippin (2021c).

the way she did; or that an apparently normal young man would, with no comprehensible motive, murder a couple and an entire family, and then suddenly turn himself in to the police. It makes no sense to me to suggest that we should just remain content with our "emotional" response and leave the matter there, especially since emotions have determinate intentional contents, they assume a construal of what is being responded to. Second, there is all the difference in the world between viewing the film, especially for the first time, and subsequent re-viewings of, reflections on, conversations about, even investigations of the film.[20] Some films, all great films, are made to be experienced several times, as are great novels and poems and artworks. Bresson is not arbitrarily choosing the music of Jean-Baptiste Lully's seventeenth-century opera *Atys* in several crucial scenes of *Pickpocket*, or Monteverdi's *Magnificat* at the opening and closing of *Mouchette*, but he hardly expects a viewer to recognize either immediately. (He knows how risky this is: "I wonder if my films are worth the effort they require" [Bresson 2013, 196].) And third, Bresson was himself willing to write about why he made his films as he did (his *Notes on the Cinematograph*), and it would be equally strange to charge *him* with reducing his films to the mere "expression of his ideas." We still have a lot of interpreting and careful watching to do to understand what he means by such claims as that cited above, that "one recognizes the true by its efficacy, its power" (*NC*, xx), especially what he means by "the true." This all obviously requires a much more fine-grained attention to the details of the films, but the general point is an important one and often very poorly understood.[21]

Bresson was an articulate, widely read intellectual who gave a number of interviews over the course of his career, and in many he was quite forthcoming about why he made his cinematographs as he did, and, like all serious artists, considerably less forthcoming about the "meaning" of his films. In 1975 he published a collection of notes and aphorisms he had been compiling over the years, *Notes on the Cinematograph*. He touched

20. This is another distinction Burnett (2023) does not note. Reflective commentary on a film need not try simply to record what one feels in watching a film—see Burnett's claims about Bresson's films working by stimulating "feelings"—but to comment on the significance of such feelings, the point of the "stimulation."

21. If Burnett (2023, and see also 2021) wants us to understand Bresson's films in this way—"This is what we encounter in Bresson's films: life-rhythms which press upon our own, edifying our sense of distinct life-types in the world we live in"—he owes us some sense of what he means by "edifying," and if he attempts to make good on that promissory note, as far as I can understand what that would mean, he will be doing what he accuses me of doing.

there on all the distinctive formal features that have come to be associated with his films.[22]

By far the most well-known directorial decision was, beginning with his casting of Claude Laydu in his 1951 film *Diary of a Country Priest*, to avoid professional actors and to cast unknowns as his major characters, nonprofessionals whom he would never use again in any other roles.[23] (Several other unknowns in later films also had careers as actors, although Bresson preferred that they not.) His summary account of this was that these unknowns were to be understood not as actors, but as "models," in the sense that one would speak of a painter or a photographer using models for his work. As he put it: "No actors. (No directing of actors.) No parts. (No learning of parts). No staging. But the use of working models taken from life. BEING (models) instead of SEEMING (actors)" (*NC*, 6). Bresson explains his decision by expressing skepticism that film actors can succeed in doing what they are asked to do. "The actor: 'It's not me you are seeing and hearing, but *the other man*.' But being unable to be wholly *the other*, he is not that other" (*NC*, 31). This is because "a CINEMA film reproduces the reality of the actor, at the same time as that of the man he is being" (*NC*, 63). Bresson clearly believes it is impossible to submerge the former into the latter; we always see both.[24]

By contrast, what would it mean to instruct a model not to "act, to ask them instead to repeat a scene and a line reading endlessly so as to discourage expressiveness"?[25] Bresson's answers to this question more and more disclose the intertwining of aesthetic and philosophical commitments, just as we would expect. A view about what is necessary in order to avoid falseness in the *depiction* of what human mindedness and attempts at communication involve, or "are really like," to attempt to avoid, as he noted above, seeming,

22. To state the obvious: nothing from the *Notes* can replace detailed attention to each frame of the films themselves. They are, as some have noted, "working" notes, and hardly a manifesto. And, also obviously, nothing guarantees that Bresson succeeds in doing what he proposes to do.

23. The one exception is Jean-Claude Guilbert, who appeared in both *Au hasard, Balthazar* and *Mouchette*. Laydu came to Paris to study acting in 1948, but he was only twenty when he was introduced to Bresson by the filmmaker Jacques Becker and had almost no experience and no film work. He agreed to Bresson's request to live for some weeks in a monastery, but not to discontinue his acting career. He ended up a children's television presenter.

24. He apparently believed that the physical reality of the stage actor in front of a live audience decreased the likelihood of this sense of the duality in personae. See Bresson's remarks (2013), x, and in his interview with Godard and Delahaye (1998), 464.

25. Bresson (2013) says he is out to "guide" his models, "to ask them to behave and not to act." "Speak as if you are speaking to yourself," xiii.

fantasy, theater, and to depict social being as it is, must involve some determinate commitment to *how* it really is, what in the simplest sense "reality" could *look like* on camera and recording. And his report of his instructions to his models makes clear that he has strong views about mindedness itself: "Radically suppress *intentions* in your models" (*NC*, 13). This will result in an apparent automatism in line delivery and expression. "Nine-tenths of our movements obey habits and automatism. It is anti-nature to subordinate them to will and to thought" (*NC*, 17). He wants to achieve this (which he does by "directing" his models about how not to act and by shooting scenes dozens and dozens of times to insure a merely habitual line reading) because of some quite general views that will require attention to the films to understand fully. "Models mechanized externally, internally free. On their faces, nothing willful. '*The constant, the eternal, beneath the accidental*'" (*NC*, 33).[26] Bresson obviously does not believe that in ordinary life people communicate with each other in an affectless, monologic, robotic way, but he clearly does believe that *on camera and as recorded*, the suppression of deliberate or visibly intentional expressiveness, and the use of minimalist voice inflection, will allow the camera and tape to record something the human eye misses in rapid normal interchanges and that this can be psychologically disclosive; aspects of the soul will, in essence, "leak out."[27] And again, what the camera and recorder capture is not what would invite recognition on the part of movie viewers. The radicality of the scope of what Bresson finds false in filmed theater is what occasions so much confusion. ("On the watch for the most imperceptible, the most inward movements" [*NC*, 26]. "Make visible what, without you, might perhaps never have been seen" [*NC*, 50].) And as he expands the thought:

> Your models, pitched into the action of your film, will get used to gestures they have repeated twenty times. The words they have learned with their lips will find, *without their minds taking part in this*, the inflections and the lilt proper to their true natures. A way of recovering the automatism of real life. (The talent of one or several actors or stars no longer comes into it.

26. I take this contrast to be between the human condition as it is in itself and the particular experience of that condition in a particular historical world.

27. Moravia's strange description actually gets at it well: "The actors play their roles with hallucinatory sobriety" (Moravia 1998), 408. Cf. what Bresson says in his interview with Godard: "When I think that someone says to me that in my films people speak falsely! Me, I would have people speak falsely! But what makes that person believe that he himself speaks rightly?" Godard and Delahaye (1998), 467.

> What matters is how you approach your models and the unknown and the virgin nature you manage to draw from them.) (*NC*, 42)

Another way to put the point has been well stated by Michael Haneke. He argues that traditional expressionistic acting

> robbed the viewers of this professional reproduction of their most precious possession as viewers: their imagination. They were forced into the humiliating perspective of a voyeur at the keyhole who has no choice but to feel what is being felt before him and think what is being thought. (Haneke 2010, 569)

The keyhole image is apt. In traditional cinema, we are prompted to indulge one of the oldest human fantasies, one that goes back to Plato's Gyges's ring story. We think of ourselves as observing unobserved, invisible, and thereby onto some truth, not what would be pretended if we were acknowledged. But this is the illusion of reality, the great trick of traditional cinema, and it encourages laziness and passivity on the part of the viewer. Haneke puts this well too.

> Cinema has missed out on the opportunity it has, new in comparison with literature, to represent reality as a total sensory impression, to develop forms that maintain and even for the first time enable the necessary dialog between a work of art and its recipient. The lie that pretense is reality has become the trademark of cinema—one of the most profitable in the annals of industry. (Haneke 2010, 569)

Another way to put this is that what the camera and sound recording can capture is the extent to which characters, especially when they attempt to or are instructed to hold themselves back, not reveal anything, nevertheless give themselves away, reveal themselves.[28]

In the following we will have to explore what Bresson means by "true natures" or "virgin nature," a first formulation of his claim to philosophical truth, but for now we should note that Bresson cannot make the claims he does without a commitment to some very broad views about human mindedness, agency, and sociality, as well as, for many commentators, free

28. See Jones's (1998) compelling remark: "Only Bresson makes the ceaseless self-revelation of people both the central event and the lynchpin of his cinema," 93.

will, transcendence, faith, and grace. None of this means that the films are vehicles for the expression of these views. The films are the views.

With respect to his skepticism about actors, he is clearly suspicious that a wide range of meaningful comportment with objects in the world and with others is (originally or as Heidegger is wont to say, primordially) conceptually self-conscious or at all cognitive, and suspicious as well that actions we perform are always best understood by reference to the intentions we would self-consciously avow. That is, his suspicion of movie acting reflects a suspicion that why we do what we do is best understood by what intentions we would explicitly express when asked why we are so acting. The claim is not that there are no intentions, but that our avowals are not trustworthy, even if sincere. This may be true in most cases, of course, but the situation is usually more complicated in critical or decisive situations. "Models who have become automatic . . . their relations with objects and persons around them will be *right*, because they will not be *thought*" (*NC*, 17). I suggest that he does not merely mean "will seem right on camera because not acted out" but because it avoids a false view of the too confident role of self-conscious "thought" in our ordinary familiarity with objects and persons in the world and in our actions.

In turn, this implies something much broader: that at the original or primordial level of our experience, simply how things show up as salient in our world, the availability of being, is first of all a matter of what he calls "impressions and sensations." I think that what he is getting at will require a more perspicacious language than impressions and sensations,[29] which can suggest mere affects causally produced (which is not at all what he means; he is not pleading for empiricism or behaviorism), and I will introduce a broader account in the next section. But what he is after is clear enough when he gives this advice about shooting a scene—"Stick exclusively to sensations. No intervention of intelligence which is foreign to these impressions and sensations" (*NC*, 24)—again because the intention in shooting this way is to capture how it is, not how it seems.[30] He is committing himself here to something quite controversial: that there is a mode of nondiscursive intelligibility by virtue of which the world and indeed our own being in such a world are originally familiar and meaningful, that is, significant. The question he wants to raise is not about mere perceptual availability.

29. "We shouldn't look for truth in facts, in beings or things ('realism,' as it's generally construed, does not exist), but in the emotions they provoke. Emotional truth is what teaches and guides us." Bresson (2013).

30. Often Bresson does not seem to appreciate the great diagnostic value and great difficulty in capturing how it seems, the specialty of Hollywood cinema.

One technique Bresson uses to emphasize this modality is his emphasis on hands at work, paradigmatically in *Pickpocket* and *A Man Escaped*, but hardly limited to these. By greatly limiting usual sequences like shots of hands at work followed by close-ups of intense faces, and concentrating instead on the hands alone, Bresson manages to portray the hands as agents of intelligence themselves, a "minded" *hand*, where mindedness is the easy and nondiscursive know-how evident in it being at work.[31]

This is a level of meaningfulness prior to perceptual and conceptual discriminability. Likewise, the camera must try to capture a relation between an agent and her deeds that is not limited to the conscious intentions that the agent would avow. For example, Bresson wants to deny that the effect of his directorial instructions produces *in*expressiveness: "Involuntarily expressive models (not willfully inexpressive ones)." And "no psychology of the kind which discovers only what it can explain." "*When you do not know what you are doing* and what you are doing is the best—that is inspiration." What he is after is clear enough when he gives this advice about shooting a scene—"Stick exclusively to sensations. No intervention of intelligence which is foreign to these impressions and sensations"—all again, because the intention in shooting this way is to capture how it is, not how it seems, how persons might believe it is.

This takes a position on the fundamental basic availability of a meaningful world of objects and others: that it is nondiscursively and precognitively available, that elements of a world become originally salient to us in their meaningfulness or mattering, and that we are onto any such meaning by being attuned to it in a way that parallels our unreflective absorption in a filmed world, if such meaningful directionality to a life *is* available to a character. This claim about the nondiscursive availability of the world and of others is, I want to show, the most fundamental feature of Bresson's cinematic innovations. By nondiscursive, I mean to deny (with Bresson) that our original experience of the world is of "propositionally shaped" objects, content that can always be formulated in propositional form. That is the significance of the notion of "attunement" (*Stimmung* in Heidegger) noted above. And this is not as radical a philosophical claim as it might appear. We find it easily credible to say that one knows someone who really "understands" Sati or Mozart or Schönberg, where one doesn't mean understands counterpoint or diatonic theory, and we can say that we can "see" that someone claiming something about themselves is self-deceived, or that

31. Cf. the discussion of hands in Price (2002a), and especially his contrast between films like *A Man Escaped* and the depiction of hands in *L'Argent*.

we "knew right away" that someone was on the same wave length as we are, all of which appeal to this everyday notion of attunement. And again, ultimately this entails something even more controversial philosophically: that a filmed fictional narrative can, given this modality of availability, disclose something true about the human world, without such a truth being statable in a proposition.

His general philosophical commitments are also implied in positions he takes on how to understand, both for credible cinematic representations and in themselves, the relation between inner mindedness and outer comportment, as well as the general bearing of psychology as usually understood in understanding what we do. His remarks about this issue are often quite sweeping and so brief as to be gnomic at times.[32] They will require detailed attention to the films to understand. It is in the films that his real philosophical reflection takes place.

> The real, when it has reached the mind is already not real any more. Our too thoughtful, too intelligent eye. [This is a Proustian thought, to which we shall often return.]
>
> Two sorts of real (1) the crude real as recorded by the camera; (2) what we call real and see deformed by our memory and some wrong reckonings.
>
> Problem: To make real what you have seen, through the intermediary of a machine that does not see it as you see it. (*NC*, 48)

This suspicion of "intelligence," self-consciousness, avowed intentions as all surface phenomena, as only superficially making sense of our conduct and exchanges with objects and persons, is expressed as the cinematic intention to de-emphasize a "psychology of consciousness" and to reverse our usual assumptions about the relation between inner and outer.[33] Hence some of the aphorisms. "No psychology (of the kind which discovers only what it can explain"). Or in his fullest but still quite telegraphic statement:

> Movement from the exterior to the interior. (Actors: movement from the interior to the exterior.)
>
> The thing that matters is not what they show me but what they hide from me and above all, what they do not suspect is in them. (*NC*, 6)

32. This is a Bressonian theme particularly prominent in the work of the Dardenne brothers, obviously much influenced by Bresson. See Pippin (2020b).

33. This approach naturally invites psychoanalytic interest, as in Tony Pipolo's well-known study (2010).

At the most straightforward level, Bresson means that *what the camera shows us and what can be recorded* on a soundtrack, in a character's face, demeanor, reactions, silences, as contrasted with the outer expressions of what a character (or an actor) *consciously inwardly means to express* or even takes himself to be feeling, are more trustworthy and credible on film than the effects of an actor's intentional staging of such mindedness or our own intentional attempts to communicate expressively.[34] But this, like many of the cinematic decisions, would not be the case were it not also true that we simply misunderstand what it is for an agent to be "in" her deed, to be the author of it, to be expressive, if we think of her as in effect controlling the meaning of the deed or the emotional valence produced by what she would be willing to avow as her intention. What it means not to be so in control is not, as we shall see, for the characters presented actually to *be* automatons, the mere plaything of psychic forces over which they have no control, as if the idea were to deny any role for "the inner" in our account of ourselves. The idea is to complicate any simple or straightforward "inner-outer" model in our comprehension of ourselves and others. In films like *Diary of a Country Priest* or *Pickpocket*, which involve voiced-over diary entries, what the character takes himself to be up to is not meant to be revealed as all surface phenomena and therefore dispensable. But the pairing or doubling of the subject's descriptions and self-analysis with what we see of the subject's deeds and comportment is meant to complicate the picture of any "inner direction of the outer."

So Bresson is obviously confident that his use of nonprofessionals and the comparatively flat effects of his directorial instructions (such as making the nonactor repeat the line interminably just in order to "flatten" that effect) will still produce a powerful emotional punch, no matter how different his cinematographs look from movies. This is partly because, I am suggesting, his films reflect views about the general (and generally unnoticed or screened, forgotten) availability of meaningfulness in a human world, and thus the sources of possible meaningfulness, that are both philosophically credible and attested to by the films themselves. That is in itself a controversial issue. But he also has this confidence because of what he believes a cinematograph is. A typical definition:

34. Bresson goes to extraordinary lengths to achieve this "involuntary expressiveness." In postproduction, when post-synchronization of the soundtrack is necessary, rather than doing so with the actor watching the scene and trying to recover the dialogue that must be inserted, Bresson's models sit in a darkened room with earphones on, repeating after Bresson, sometimes twenty or thirty times, the lines he wants recorded.

> Cinematographic film, where expression is obtained by relations of images and of sounds, and not by a mimicry done with gestures and intonations of voice (whether actors' or non-actors'). One that does not analyze or explain. That *recomposes*. (*NC*, 9)

As the name implies, Bresson means to compare his method of composition to writing with images, where images are not understood as represented contents so much as acquiring meaning in sequences of images. (As in linguistic holism, where the basic unit of meaning is not the word but the sentence.) "Cinematography: A new way of writing, therefore of feeling" (*NC*, 21). Or:

> An image must be transformed by contact with other images, as is a color by contact with other colors. A blue is not the same blue beside a green, a yellow, a red. No art without transformation. (*NC*, 21)

This is to produce a "cinema of montage and rhythm," one that is "primarily poetry and music, the creation of new relationships between things, beings, sounds and images, as in the succession of shots."[35] This notion of Bresson relying so heavily on image sequences can be taken too far, though. Bresson's films are not like silent films without intertitles and disconnected images; they are fictional narrative films, with plots, dialogue, and beginnings, middles, and ends. The images, the individual shots, have content, and the link between the shots—that is, the comprehensibility of the sequences—depends heavily on some continuity of sense among these contents as well as what Bresson is emphasizing by appealing to cinematography: an atmospheric emotional coloring built from montage, the sequence itself.[36] This goes considerably beyond Lev Kuleshov's famous experiments with montage and its impact upon the interpretation of imagery, since Bresson is assuming that his sequences of images can build to create a noncognitive attunement to matters of significance and meaningfulness not otherwise available. So sequences of shots often do not follow conventional narrative montage; there are few shots of classic sequences like, for example, crying child, then dying mother, then worried father. Instead, someone might look off camera, and then rather than showing the viewer what he was looking

35. Prédal (1998), 75.

36. So Sitney's assertion (1998, 162) that there is a heavy emphasis on meaning as figural in Bresson must be correct, but he goes too far when he says, "The space of Bresson's fictions is a trap for capturing meaning, which, for him, is *always* figural" (my emphasis).

at, we see a shot of legs and feet moving along a sidewalk. The point is not randomness but the disruption of normal expectations and the creation of a different tonality than is conventional, one that contributes to rather than is independent of what happens on screen. And it is a reminder that while Sontag is right that form is meaning in Bresson, it goes too far to say that meaning is exclusively form.[37]

But he is clearly reducing the informational content of these images, stripping down what is visually available in the "material" of the shot, refraining from establishing shots in a way that creates the impression of closed-in interiors, often an almost prisonlike (or literal prison) atmosphere. In the same way, he is minimalizing what we learn about characters from the dialogue and especially what we might use in attempting psychological explanations. We spend ninety-five minutes with the priest in *Diary of a Country Priest*, and we learn nothing about his childhood,[38] his family, his native region, his path to the priesthood, his seminary experience, and only once, at the very end, about any friendships at the seminary. Much the same could be said about all the major characters.[39]

Several other cinematic properties are also connected to philosophical commitments. His mostly stationary camera (very few pans), 50 mm lens[40] (the closest to the focus of the human eye), static framing, medium shots, a "flat" photographic effect, always "bounced" lighting, very few uses of nondiegetic music, the air of stillness, the use of silences, and incongruities between cinematic framing and narrative importance all suggest a complete cinematic neutrality, coldness, unemotional suppression of meaning

37. See Price (2007) on Sontag and Bresson. Hayward (1986) goes into quite useful detail about how sequences in Bresson's montage work, as when the sense of one scene is given by a former (anaphora), or by a later (cataphora), or is left without such resolution (exophera). Her detailed account of his uses of elision and ellipsis is also very helpful.

38. We know a bit more in the novel: that he grew up in poverty and great misery. See Curran (2006), 23.

39. As noted, there has always been a great deal of discussion about Bresson's objections to filmed theater. But Rancière (2014) makes an interesting point about how *The Diary* differs from Bernanos's literary treatment: "For example, Bresson removed the wealth of sensory detail in the meeting with the Count on his return from a day's hunting, carrying a pile of dead, muddy and bloody rabbits but out of which one animal's gentle eye seemed to be staring back at the priest. A naturally visual art, cinema had to reduce the excess of visual imagery that literature used to project itself in imagination beyond its own powers. Hence the quintessential character of the film, carrying the literary narrative to a higher level of abstraction," 21.

40. There is apparently one exception, the opening shot of the scarf falling in *Une femme douce*, a shot that Bresson reported took sixty takes. See Burnett and Hourigan's discussion: Burnett (2004), 11–12.

for the sake of what appears to be mere perceptual materiality. (As in the first scenes of *A Man Escaped*, when Fontaine leaps out of the car trying to escape and the camera does not even follow him, stays in the car with the other two prisoners, who, bafflingly, do not react or even look.) This leveling of significance, where the camera does not indicate anything of more importance than any other has suggested to some a kind of documentary realism, but it is not what Fried has called an "ocular" realism.[41] (The ordinary human world does not look like, "feel" like, the Bressonian film world.) Rather his is a kind of ontological realism, a depiction of what we are left with—and I want to insist, what we are left with *now*, that the Bressonian world is very much historically indexed—when the fantasy, the theater, is removed, stripped away.[42] By ontological realism I mean that Bresson is trying to find a way of recording something like the basic or essential distinctiveness of the human experiential path through a life, and this in several registers: children, adolescents, priests, villagers, saints, knights, Parisian youths. To get to what he wants to disclose, he strips away a great deal of what movies traditionally rely on, self-reflection, self-justifications, and self-avowals. Absent such markers of a character's identity, their understanding of each other and their treatment of each other both demand formal means unique in cinema, one where the barest hint of a reaction, a motorcycle ride, a long moment of silence, the slow, patient, carrying out of task, a hand on a seat, a moment in a church, a counterfeit bill, all by virtue of this minimalism, carry a weight of possible meaning that is absent in conventional cinema, even though just that minimality can also make its appearance in the film mysterious, opaque, elusive, requiring what existence itself requires, attempts at interpretation that in the reticence of these films, can cause irritation and impatience on the part of viewers.

These formal/cinematic properties—the minimalism, austerity of visual information, slow narrative pacing, minimalization of "action," "depsychologization"—create a much commented on paradox, what has been called "making art by eliminating art."[43] The minimalization of expressed emotion can paradoxically create an even more powerful emotional charge

41. Fried (1992).

42. As Bresson puts it: "cinema copies life or photographs it, while for me I recreate life staring from elements in as natural, as crude a state as possible." Godard and Delahaye (1998), 474. Bresson seems aware of the similarities between his intentions and Cézanne's. "*Equality of all things*. Cézanne painting with the same eye and the same soul a fruit dish, his son, Montagne St. Victoire." *NC*, 86. The effect of such discipline is to suggest the attempt to paint, to film, being qua being, the meaning of being. For more discussion of the relation, see Doebler (2006).

43. Prédal (1998), 77.

to the scenes than conventional expressivism; the reduction of meaningful information can create the impression of intense, deep meaningfulness just by its visual absence and the implied intensity and questions this creates; a camera lingering on an empty scene just vacated by a character can create a sense of mystery about the relation between place and character. Lingering shots of stairwells and open or closed doors come to be linked with the imprisoned/liberated tonality created by the absence of broad establishing shots. The way objects (wine, bread, mattresses, watches, dresses, motorbikes, cars, books, money) and body parts (hands, legs, feet) are photographed can embody a comprehensive ontology of beings in their world, in their distinctive mode of availability within a lived human world. ("I would like to create both a film of objects and a film of the soul; that is, attain the latter through the former.")[44] So, in effect, Rosenbaum is right to claim that Bresson is more correctly called an "essentialist" rather than a minimalist.[45] These techniques all also involve the creation of an implied meaningfulness or importance that the viewer can be "onto" or appreciate that is not the result of discursive interpretation, and that will be an important element in the next section.

I said before that Bresson withholds from us information about a character that might tempt us to some psychological understanding but that is not quite right. Rather than withholding anything, Bresson is attesting to how little can ever be known about a character, even by the character him- or herself, that the basic condition of human interchange is unknowingness and at best uncertainty.[46] As we shall see, there will be many cases in the films of actions that seem unmotivated, even gratuitous. This is especially true of acts of cruelty or violence, but also, as in *L'Argent*, of unimaginable kindness and generosity. But the impression created on the viewer is not mere senselessness but mystery and an intimation of motivation that must exist but remains persistently obscure, hidden but partly available. As noted before, he always suggests that mutual understanding within the fictional world and between the viewer and the fictional world is not a matter of mere or exclusive behavioral "outsides" but of the *primacy* of outer manifestations in intimating, in varying and always cloudy ways, signs of elusive inwardness, the meaning of which is inseparable from its outer manifestation in a social world.[47]

44. Reported by Amédée Ayfre, cited in Prédal (1998), 85.

45. Rosenbaum (1998), 19.

46. For a fuller discussion of this condition and its appearance on film, see Pippin (2017).

47. I think we will see that Prédal must be quite wrong when he claims "Bresson is defending a behavioral psychology of which cinema seems to be particularly effective" (1998), 80.

All of these formal matters bear on the treatment of the existential themes in the films, loneliness, deracination, solitude, the near impossibility of genuine communication, the sources of commitment or the failures of such commitment, and the possibility of radical conversion in a life, but the way they bear and so the treatment of the themes should await a detailed look at the films.

I have called this a philosophical reappraisal and mentioned Heidegger on nondiscursive intelligibility as a particularly apt framework. But the films are not mere vehicles for philosophy, Heidegger's or anyone else's. The claim is that Bresson's marshaling of so many distinctive formal cinematic properties is in the service of an exploration of the possible sources of meaningfulness in human life in Western societies in the second half of the twentieth century. That is, the films explore what meager sources of shared senses of general significance are presupposed in a late modern world, how these are available, and what the implications are of such poverty, especially how the world we have created allows and sustains certain forms of mindedness that conceal characteristics of such a world. These include but, I want especially to claim, are not limited to, religious experiences, or what are sometimes referred to as experiences of "transcendence." To do so, he obviously is assuming, taking a position on, the nature of that question and what factors are relevant in addressing it in a distinctly cinematic way.

The films direct our attention to such large issues, and in great seriousness. They allow us to see either such orientability or its absence in the individual projects of the characters. These would include such themes as the priest's religious convictions and the hostile reactions of the villagers in *Diary of a Country Priest*; the meaning and importance of freedom in *A Man Escaped*; the meaning of law and crime in *Pickpocket*; how rapid economic and technological change affects traditional hierarchies of importance in *Au hasard, Balthazar*; the importance accorded (or not) to family life and community in *Mouchette* (and in these last two and several other films, how people experience the significance of and place of sexual desire in a human life); what political conviction means, how it could matter, in contemporary Paris in *The Devil, Probably*; and the significance of money in *L'Argent*.[48]

Stated this way, the topic is still vague and could include almost anything and everything in almost any film or narrative about a human life, and such attentiveness could wrongly suggest that the point of the films is the making of a philosophical point. What I am trying to suggest is a specific *framework*

48. The historical films, like *The Trial of Joan of Arc* and *Lancelot du Lac*, would require a separate discussion.

for an interpretation of the films, a philosophical language that can be interpretively helpful, one that will take some time here to set out and that will require amplification in terms of the details of the film. That framework is no doubt already apparent to anyone familiar with Martin Heidegger and his understanding of the problem of the "*Sinn des Seins*," the meaning of being question, as he set it out in his university lectures in the 1920s and 1930s and in his unfinished masterpiece of 1927, *Being and Time*.[49] The following summation will have to be quite telegraphic, and I only want to say enough to make clear the general framework invoked and to clarify some of the terminology, like world, being-in-the-world, attunement, significance, the limitations of discursivity, and so forth. And I won't be referring to Heidegger in explicit detail and will concentrate on the films. But this should be enough to begin such an interpretation, keeping in mind all the while the problems of potential anachronism, of forcing the films to speak a language alien to them, and of ignoring the uniqueness of distinctly cinematic reflections of the problems.

However, in the case of Bresson, whose films clearly aspire to a level of seriousness and ambition on a philosophical scale beyond issues of cinematic aesthetics, Heidegger can be particularly helpful. This is because he advances the most ambitious claim about aesthetic truth in the history of philosophy, and indeed about nonpropositional, nondiscursive truth itself. Heidegger claims that art and, I want to say in extension of his claims, specifically cinema[50] should be considered forms of philosophical or poetic *thinking*,[51] and while they do not consist of propositions asserted, can nevertheless disclose something true and even indispensable to some more capacious notion of philosophy than is standard in the academy. As Heidegger puts it in an essay called "Why Poetry" (where poetry stands in for art in general and can easily be taken to refer to Bresson's poetic cinema):

> Admittedly, the first thing we must learn at this moment of world history is that making poems is also a matter of thinking. We will take the poem as a practice exercise in poetic reflection.

Heidegger is well known as an "existentialist," but those issues make up a minor and very early part of his philosophical project. In his 1927 lecture

49. I defend the interpretation of Heidegger sketched here and the claim for its significance for philosophy in Pippin (2024).

50. Admittedly, this extension is not something that would be welcomed by Heidegger, whose aversion to technology in the arts led to several skeptical statements about photography and cinema.

51. On the idea of poetic thinking, see Pippin (2024), 205–20.

course, *The Basic Problems of Phenomenology*, Heidegger is unambiguous about what he considers *the* basic philosophical problem. "We assert now that being is the proper and sole theme of philosophy" (*BPP*, 11). Philosophy itself is said to be "the science of being" (*BPP*, 13). That Heidegger believes this is unambiguous. But the issue is made difficult because Heidegger is eager to qualify and to some extent marginalize the usual philosophical approaches, for example, very familiar semantic ways of addressing the problem: the various senses of the word "is." Moreover, it is not just linguistic or semantic meaning that Heidegger excludes as his topic. That is why his issue is so hard to get a handle on. If the question is "the meaning of Being," it would seem natural to begin by appreciating that *meaning* is what we understand in attending to another's or a text's words, or that meaning is what we come to understand when someone's actions seem unintelligible to us until we learn what her ends are and her intentions to achieve it. Or meaning is understood in an intentionality context where it means determinate content, the meaning of something intended *as* something, such as consciousness being onto a determinate content. Then we say we understand the meaning of what she is saying or what she is doing or we understand a determinate content of an intention.

It would therefore seem natural to understand the question as asking what someone means to say when he says something exists or declares the meaning of some action, declares it *to be what it is*, *that* action or that someone is aware of that object as such and such, some determinate content is present to the mind and in that sense "is." Because it is understood as just *that* such and such, it is meaningful, in the sense of intelligible. If we respond that Heidegger always considers that such formulations still leave the basic question unclarified, then again we might think he wants to ask "what it means to be at all" in this semantic or intentional sense of meaning. But he tells us that such formulations assume the answer to the question he is trying to pose, and so do not point to a way of addressing it. It assumes the question is about the criterion of existence, and that already means *whether* something is present-at-hand or present, as he will say, or as in "a determinate content as such" as present to consciousness.

Moreover, if Heidegger's lifelong claim is that forgetting the question of the meaning of being is a catastrophic event in the history of mankind, that it leads to nihilism and a predatory, self-destructive technical manipulation of the earth, then it is extremely hard to see how one could claim that this has come about because we do not have an adequate account of what we mean when we say that anything is. The forgetting of the meaning of being is, he says, "the age of complete meaning*less*ness." So, any retrieval of the question must be a path toward a renewed attention to the meaning*ful*ness of being. Accordingly, we must keep in mind that in any of Heidegger's formulations about the "problem of Being," he doesn't mean by his question, "What is the meaning of our existence," where that question is most often taken to mean things like "Why are we here?" "What is the point of a human life?" "How should a human being live in order to live well?" In the first place, he argues that these questions already distort the basic issue by assuming that a human being is a kind of thinglike being, a kind of substance, for whom such questions are possible. ("What is it for?")

I suggest we take our bearings by passages like this one in *Being and Time*:

> Significance is that on the basis of which the world is disclosed as such. (*BT*, 182)

> Bedeutsamkeit ist das, woraufhin Welt als solche erschlossen ist. (*SZ*, 143)

It is this notion of *Bedeutsamkeit*, or meaningfulness, that is at the heart of the question he wants to reanimate. This has several dimensions. It starts with a rejection of the post-Cartesian view of a representing subject confronting an objective world, and the subsequent question of how a subject could ever with any certainty know that its representations correspond with the way things are. Rather than a subject-object picture, Heidegger argues that, phenomenologically, human being, which he calls Dasein, is always already a being-in-the-world, a particular historical world into which we find ourselves simply "thrown." With such a notion as primary or originary, Heidegger notes that our fundamental experience in the world is a kind of immediate familiarity with what we encounter (or more in line with the being-in-the-world idea, that we are always already familiar with our world), what is available to encounter, as meaningful, and not as objects the relations to which we must establish. As we walk into a kitchen and begin preparing a meal, we understand what we encounter not by representing objects and their properties, but by practically understanding how to use the utensils and food we simply take up and work on. And what is salient in any experience is an issue of this sort of practical attentiveness—salient in the sense that we do not notice in that kitchen as we cook, even though we may perceive, the car keys on the counter, or the electricity bill. In that context, those do not matter, given our practical comportments (what we are on about, trying to do), in the context in terms of which beings are originally available in everyday life. What is important here, and what links Heidegger so deeply with Bresson, is the rejection of a picture of such availability in which the easy and immediate familiarity we experience in the world is fundamentally or originally a matter of perception and conceptual clarification. The working out through what Bresson calls "intelligence," or self-conscious discrimination, is secondary to the way the world makes its primary sense to us in the course of our various comportments as well as in our dealings with others. Moreover, if this is true, then this fundamental level of intelligibility is a prediscursive or noncognitive mode of availability. Things are salient (or not) in our experience by virtue of how they matter, both how they matter given some particular task we are about, and by virtue of a world of possible significance at a historical time. Think only of the silent intensity of Fontaine's constructing the tools he needs to escape in *A Man Escaped*, the project in terms of which bed sheets, blankets, lantern frames, bed springs, or spoons acquire a meaning all their own, show up for him in terms of that project, not originally as their perceptual properties or other uses. Or Michel perfecting his thieving technique in *Pickpocket*; or the meaning of bread and wine, the nature of their salience, for the priest in *Diary of a Country Priest*; or what transistor radios and motorbikes mean to Gérard in *Au hasard, Balthazar*; and especially how Bresson in all these cases focuses our attention on these objects in which he manages to convey both this aura of meaningfulness and the world in which they could become so meaningful or fail to be. This world is an interconnected network of interrelated significances. The utensils, food, spices are all "for the sake of" each other in a way that is already in play as we execute some culinary task. We don't "project" such significances onto physical things or "decide" on their importance because we are never in an ex ante position of facing physical objects onto which we project; we are always already in a world of such significances.

And we are "onto" such matterings not by a conceptualization of what matters but by what Heidegger calls "attunement" (*Stimmung*), in, as the term implies, just the way musical instruments can be said to be attuned to one another, or in which two people find "they are on the same wave length," attuned to each other in taste and preferences, all without being experienced as a set of propositions or beliefs that account for such attunement. Those formulations are possible (at least in a rough general way), but they do not comprise what the attunement originally consists in—are not primary but secondary. (Recall all those passages cited above in which Bresson complains about the distorting effects of "intelligence" and "self-consciousness.") Moreover, this notion that the primary availability of any being is not discursive or conceptual, even though obviously some perceptual and discriminatory capacities are necessary conditions enabling such availability through salient significance, in the same way that having a functioning brain and respiratory system is. And this means that our experience of any such horizon of possible sense (the "world") is not a *result* of beliefs held about what ought to matter or what not. Some things matter to some people and not to others, but what is important to Heidegger is that they find themselves caring about what they care about, and they are not the subjects of what could matter at a time but subject to such possibilities. It is easy to imagine someone having a number of beliefs about what ought to matter to her, and even taking steps to realize such beliefs, while knowing that they do not matter to her in the way that, say, reputation or convention matter. Or, as noted earlier, someone who is embarrassed by what matters to him, feels it shouldn't, but knows it nevertheless still does.

This form of nondiscursive understanding is another mark of the potential value of cinematic experience, since, in keeping with this general view, which I have suggested through quotations from *NC*, as viewers *our* attentiveness, anxieties, concern, hostility, uncertainty, and so forth are not engaged as a result of any assessment but are direct features of our immediate absorption in a cinematic world. (Bresson's word for attunement is "emotional.") And this is how he portrays being-in-the-world in his films. No even moderately sensitive viewer can think that Balthazar has no standing as anything other than a tool, a thing, but the people who treat him that way, who do not see him as a living being with his own mode of appropriate and inappropriate (unnatural) engagement with his animal world, also themselves live in a world changing in a way in which such a distinction (between meaning and thingness) is harder to make out, all with disastrous consequences for their treatment of each other. (Everyone becomes a means.) This surely has something to do with a world of donkey carts and a farmer's temporal pace and involvement with animals becoming a world of cars and tractors, motorbikes, transistor radios, makeup for young girls, and a circus world for animals, their becoming objects of amusement.

For Heidegger this all involves what he regards as the most important issue in the philosophical tradition, the "meaning" of being, the source of possible significance in an interrelated shared historical world. His scope here is quite broad, to say the least. He means the Western world, understood as the descendant of the ancient Greek enlightenment, culminating first in scientific modernity, and finally in the age of technology and capital, *l'argent*, ours, where meaningfulness (in the barest sense) is a matter of being material for technical manipulation or having exclusively exchange value, manipulation understood as in the service of human being, itself understood as a thing like any other. What he means by our having forgotten the question of the meaning of being can be understood in these terms. That any pre-reflective attunement to such original meaningfulness has been lost, forgotten, or at best deeply obscured, is how Heidegger wants to characterize our "destitute" time, a time of homelessness and, we shall see, a similar way of thinking about our historical world emerges in Bresson's work, even if not in these terms. Although we might disavow the claim, the meaning of being, what has come first of all to matter to us, has been reduced to the mere perceivable presence of beings, a kind of barely meaningful form of intelligibility, and is a conception that is a distortion of our original attunement to mattering, or even of who we are. Heidegger claims that the dominant understanding of Being since antiquity and because of the Greek enlightenment is what is simply present, at hand, there, extended in the present, substance, and enduring through a sequence of presents. We have convinced ourselves that beings show up because what has come to matter to us after Plato must first of all be their intelligibility, their *eidos* and thereby, not coincidentally, their manipulability. Bresson, of course, evinces no such views about the history of metaphysics and its implications, but he does present a world in which characters convince themselves of various aspects of meaningfulness in their lives (or don't even bother), but whose actions reflect a much more limited range of what matters, manifestations in line with Heidegger's general picture. The importance of conformism to convention as a source of meaning (above all in *Mouchette*), which Heidegger emphasizes in *Being and Time*, submission, he says, to *das Man*, the They, is also a point of convergence.

There are also aspects of Heidegger's interest in authenticity, what it would be to liberate oneself from convention, and thus experience one's existence as truly one's own, but not via the Heideggerian experiences of anxiety and being-toward-death. (This is quite prominent in *Pickpocket*.) The self-opacity, self-deceit, and inauthenticity of Michel in *Pickpocket* are evasions of "having one's own being at issue for oneself," as Heidegger describes it, and this is not treated as an individual moral failure but as typical.

It will be in an examination of several of the films that we will be able to see whether this framework is useful: these notions of world as a horizon of possible significance, being-in-the-world, the historical world of late modernity, the primordiality of meaningfulness, mattering, as fundamental in the availability of being, the nondiscursive, precognitive character of our understanding of such intelligibility of objects in the world and especially of each other, the role of what Heidegger calls inauthenticity or in Bresson self-deceit in the broad forgetfulness or thoughtlessness of daily modern life (and not simple sinfulness), and a kind of self-alienation that results from this forgetfulness. It is admittedly dangerous to lean too heavily on such a framework. By trying to account for the power of the films and what moves us when we watch them, we cannot ignore the purely cinematic and broadly aesthetic qualities of the films. They are, for example, beautiful, and there is an atmospheric continuity in them that marks them as Bressonian.

That beauty derives from the perfection with which form fits content in the works, and no amount of exposition can reproduce that distinctive absorption in words. So care must be exercised.

For example, Bresson's films are almost always very tightly focused on an individual, and if this appeal to Heidegger is to be of any value, then Heidegger's notion of Dasein as "being-in-the-world," or the inseparability of individual existence and historical world, must bear on what Bresson is up to. I think that can be demonstrated, for one thing simply because of what Bresson decided to make films about. And his taking his lead from authors like Dostoyevsky, Bernanos, and Tolstoy already implies some sort of crisis in the modern European world. A crisis of faith, a failure of desire, boredom, an absence of human solidarity, a fetishism of commodities, greed, the destruction of the planet, all make appearances in his films, and they all seem to have to do with a crisis in what Heidegger calls significance, *Bedeutsamkeit*, how what matters in a world generally comes to matter, and what consequences flow from such dispensations. The films are austere and minimalist, but that just increases the urgency expressed in the form he chooses. One could say that what Adorno wrote about Kafka is suggestive about the implications of reading Bresson with Heidegger in mind.

> His [Kafka's] novels, if they still at all fall under that category, are prolegomena to a condition of the world in which the contemplative attitude has become bloody mockery, because the permanent threat of catastrophe no longer permits anyone to look on passively or to tolerate the aesthetic result of such passivity.[52]

The condition of the world, I want to show, is as major a "character" in Bresson's work as the priest or Fontaine, or Michel, or Balthazar.

The first challenge in such an inquiry is one of his most difficult films, *Diary of a Country Priest*, not, I want to show, just the straightforward story of a pious, even holy young man, suffering and lost in a profane secular world.

I have obviously not attempted an overview of Bresson's oeuvre. I have selected films, hopefully a wide enough range, from different periods, that referring to them as typical of Bresson is credible. In each of the five films that I have chosen as ways to explore what Bresson means by trying to make "film as film," to quote Victor Perkins's famous book title, the focus is on a single character, the priest in *Diary*, Michel in *Pickpocket*, Marie in *Balthazar*, Mouchette in *Mouchette*, and Yvon in *L'Argent*. There are two

52. Adorno (1983), 246.

characteristics common to all of them: profound loneliness, and some mode of resistance to and rejection of, non-complicity with, the world into which they find themselves thrown. And the two are obviously connected. Bresson does not rely on the conventional means of dialogue, plot developments, characters' self-explanations, and the like to explore what it is like for these characters to locate themselves outside the ordinary or why they cannot but be alienated. But he is clearly trying to show us, by means of his unusual reliance on editing, sound, staging, silences, and pacing, the source of this homelessness in the humanly inhospitable "home" or world of postwar France, a figure for late modernity in general. The cinematic extremes that he relies on are another dimension of the reappraisal I want to defend. They are linked to the fact that his films, especially after *Pickpocket*, are far more historically indexed and historically critical than has been appreciated. And this helps account for his unusual technique as well. The "subtraction" of so many standard movie conventions allows him "to film," in effect, "what's left" of any world that could plausibly be said to provide some horizon of meaningfulness, or at least one that could inspire involvement in, commitment to what those conventions normally rely on. Likewise, his refusal to allow the viewer to rely on psychological expressiveness forces our attention on such a world ("the world worlding" as Heidegger puts it, being the world it is) and shows us modes of possible being in such a world in which available sources of meaningfulness, beyond strategic self-promotion and greed, have been thinned out to a base level. The atmosphere created cinematically in this exploration is uniformly grim, as we are exposed to various absences, what such a world lacks, different aspects of such lacks that we can sense, become attuned to, in the fate of the characters. Those various aspects of failed meaning and the assumptions at work in what is presented will be the focus of the following.

2
Justice in *Diary of a Country Priest*

Bresson's 1951 film, a financial and critical success, is adapted from Georges Bernanos's novel with the same title.[1] On the one hand, it is an extremely faithful adaptation. Almost every line we hear read out in voice-overs and in the dialogue is from the novel or is clearly based on them.[2] On the other hand, it is also quite a radical departure from the book, since Bresson eliminates a great deal, and makes no attempt to "visualize" the details of Bernanos's descriptions (which are in any event minimal). In fact, the movie "looks" nothing like what the novel presents as the village even though it is presented as the apparent visual version of a diary kept in the last year of a priest's life, a year that also happens to be his first year as a parish priest in the small village of Ambricourt. The year is 1936, although only some in the village have electricity (the priest finds that he does not), and there are few motor vehicles but plenty of horse carts. We seem to see what the

1. I will not deal here with the much-discussed issues involved in Bresson's adaptation from the novel. That has been given a full and illuminating treatment by Andrews (1981). His summary statement is quite apt: "By going beyond cinema through cinema, he [Bresson] has achieved a revolution in the ethics and potential of adaptation; he has *performed* a novel in sight and sound, not capturing his subject so much as embodying it," 37. The other locus classicus for this issue is Bazin (1998). But in his account, the sensibilities of Bernanos and Bresson are virtually identified, and the film becomes an affirmation of the priest's Christian heroism. I want to argue that that is an overreading. See also Reader's (2000) sympathies with Bazin on this film, 30–42, albeit transformed in a Derridean spirit. The best detailed comparison of the two Bernanos novels and the two Bresson films adapted from them is Curran (2006).

2. Curran (2006) provides a detailed chart, tracing the similarities and divergences, 36–47.

FIGURE 2.1

priest has written about as if it is happening in the present tense, a kind of double narration. The first scene is the diary opening, and we see that he is writing in a child's notebook, something not insignificant in a film where his one ministerial "success" is said by the soul he saved to be because of his childlike nature. There are twenty-five shots of him writing in the diary and some sixty voice-overs. (The film thus thematizes a triple representational modality: speech, writing, and photography.) Our guard goes up with the first entry. The first page we are shown is an ink blotter that looks like a Pollock painting, so our first thought turns to something like disorder, chaos (figure 2.1).

An "apparent" visual version and "seem" to see because we hear and read a record of what the priest *takes himself* to have experienced, but we are also occasionally allowed to see what he misses; things we can see but he doesn't notice. The priest, for example, writes that in his first encounters with the Count, he thinks he sees a potential friend. We can see immediately how unlikely that is.[3] And he is sometimes simply unreliable. He tells

3. We are occasionally shown something he could not have seen, like Chantal eavesdropping on his conversation with the Countess, but he does learn later that she was there and might have thereby included it in the scope of what we can presume he knows when he writes the diary, not as it is happening.

us very early on that he cannot eat meat or vegetables, and a few minutes later we see him peeling potatoes for his lunch. Then the priest writes that he sees nothing wrong in writing about his life in the village with complete frankness. Why would he think it wrong in the first place to keep a diary? (This is perhaps an indication that the priest sees himself as writing for God, and he is expressing a worried humility at daring to do so.)[4] Moreover, it is a fairly reliable rule in life that when someone says they are going to speak with great frankness, there is some reason to believe either that he thinks his auditors will not believe him, or will suspect him of dissembling, or he is unsure of his own ability to be honest, that the writer suspects that at some level they do not know themselves well enough to speak with frankness. As we soon learn, frankness is not the main issue. The priest is so naive and childlike, so lacks self-awareness, that his reports are unreliable even if subjectively frank, even those about himself. He is quite right when he writes later about himself, "I know nothing of people and I never will." (At one point later, he destroys part of the diary and thinks about destroying all of it. And many passages are crossed out. Why does one cross out passages from a private diary?)[5] And he tells us that his life in the village is completely without mystery, but in the opening scenes a sense of great mystery is indeed palpable. He appears to see an older man, whom we later learn is the Count, the village's aristocrat, embracing a younger woman, whom we later learn is his child's governess, Louise. Their faces are stern, and the ominous atmosphere is certainly mysterious, although it is obvious that they are having an affair. (It is quite obvious to us that the Count and the younger woman are in an amorous embrace, but the priest does not note that and it is a bit unclear whether it ever dawns on him.)[6] The priest is filmed from behind the bars of an iron gate, an immediate indication that he will be forever "fenced off" from the villagers, will never enter their world and perhaps will never understand it (figure 2.2).

We learn quickly that the priest has a stomach ailment of some sort, and he says he can only eat days-old bread soaked in sugary wine. (Bread and wine, and his vomiting of wine and blood, play a role in the Christological

4. It is more explicit in Bernanos's novel that the priest is imagining his diary as a conversation with God, and a record of his relation to God.

5. In the novel, the deletions are said to be about the priest's sense that God has abandoned him, and also his own suicidal tendencies.

6. The Count and Louise certainly see the priest, but there is some ambiguity about whether he sees them. We see him looking toward the right, then there is a cut to them, then a cut to him looking to the left. But we do not know how far the iron gate extends to the right or at what angle he would have to be placed to be able to see them. At any rate, his general "innocence" is not ambiguous.

FIGURE 2.2

readings of the film and perhaps in his own, perhaps suicidal, attempt to identify himself with Jesus.) Claude Laydu (the nonprofessional who played the priest)[7] carries himself with a general air of melancholy, hesitancy, often great anguish and self-doubt, the reasons for which will soon be clear. Throughout the film he encounters nothing but hostility, suspicion, outright cruelty, and indifference from the villagers, not a single sympathetic or devout soul. (The Count is not far off when he tells the priest, "The people here are malicious.") The only person who attends daily mass is Louise the governess, and she ends up being no friend of the priest. (She wants his help getting the Count's daughter Chantal out of the house and into boarding school, but she fears he will take Chantal's side and writes him a note encouraging *him* to leave.) The students in his catechism class mock and

7. As noted in the previous chapter, Laydu, a Swiss Catholic, was training to be an actor but had not yet appeared in any film. This was his first serious acting job and he prepared intensely for the role, meeting with Bresson each Sunday for a year, living in a religious community, adopting their ways, even wearing one of their old, threadbare cassocks in the film. One cannot really speak of a "performance" in Bresson's films, but the constancy of mood, subtlety of reaction, and the sheer intensity of the portrayal makes it one of the greatest in film history. See Estève (1978) for more details.

torment him (a young girl named Séraphita is particularly cruel), Chantal always attempts to undermine him and often speaks to him with contempt, and the Count treats him like a servant, insulted by any attempted involvement in the family's internal conflicts.

We learn from an aborted visit to the manor (the priest becomes weak from his illness and must break off the visit) that the Countess lives in bitter and angry isolation after the death of her young child. That initial visit will set up the most important scene in the film, a long conversation between the priest and the Countess the next time he sees her about her refusal to forgive God for taking her son. Most interpretations of the film turn on the meaning of this encounter—Bernanos's version, in effect, of the Grand Inquisitor scene in *The Brothers Karamazov*.

The priest is soon frustrated by the villagers' indifference and hostility and, as he does several times, he asks advice from a neighboring cleric, an older priest from Torcy. This priest is jaded and somewhat cynical (much more so in the novel), telling the young priest he should worry about being feared, not loved, and that his job is to keep up the moral order of the village, not to be liked or even to minister to his parishioners, to help them. From this encounter, we also learn something about the priest's ability to carry out even obvious implications of such advice. Immediately after the visit, the local cabaret owner comes to tell him that he will in a few months finally get electricity. The voice-over tells us that the priest knows he should say something to the man about the revels at his café where "boys have fun getting girls drunk," but he lacks the courage to say anything. That night he is reminded of his weakness when the party spills out under his window, and because of that he suffers what may be described either as an honest and anguished confession of his loneliness and despair or an expression of self-pity brought on by the realization that he is incapable of "enforcing" any moral order in the village. (We hear the same plaintive tone when he writes about the tormenting Séraphita, asking himself why she hates him "with such exceptional maturity.") He experiences a bit later another even more intensely painful night after he discovers that his sole churchgoer, Louise, was the one who had written him a nasty note, telling him to leave. He writes that he finds he cannot pray, however badly he wants and needs to pray. He experiences his situation as one in which he has no day-to-day support or even minimal acknowledgment of his role. He is quite right in what he tells himself. There was "nothing behind him" and all he could see in front of him, in his future in the village, was a black wall. Even prostrating himself on the floor in an act of total submission feels ineffective. He experiences only isolation and silence, descends the stairs, blows out the light in the lamp and writes that "God has left me. Of that, I am sure."

When the priest becomes ill again, the Torcy priest sends him to his friend, Dr. Delbende, an atheist with a declining practice, who concedes that the priest is quite ill, but does not offer a diagnosis, beyond saying that he has inherited alcoholism from his father and that it is "too late" to do anything about his condition. We learn later from the Torcy priest that the old doctor had not adopted modern sanitation methods, and that he has lost all his patients to younger, more modern (and more sanitary) doctors in the region. This has obviously plunged him into a deep depression.

Immediately after his "God has left me" night, he learns that Delbende has died, very likely a suicide, news that upsets him a great deal. Nevertheless, somehow that night he seems to regain his faith. As a counterpoint to the blowing out the lamp symbolism, this time he is sure he hears someone calling him and goes to his window. "Yet I knew that I would find no one." He does not. (It is in this scene that we see a foreshadowing of the dramatic final image of the film, the mysterious black cross in the background [figure 2.3].)

FIGURE 2.3

FIGURE 2.4

After he learns that Chantal has planned suicide,[8] the concerned priest revisits the manor and has a long, heated argument with the Countess, after which she accepts the death of her son and reconciles herself to God. She dies peacefully that night, but Chantal and the Count's family blame the priest for upsetting her and causing her death. The priest has received a grateful letter from the Countess that would clear him of such suspicions, but he reveals its existence to no one. Louise leaves the household the next day. Chantal has succeeded in getting rid of her and avoiding boarding school. This does not end Chantal's tormenting the priest, mocking him and telling him that the whole town thinks he is a drunk.

His illness worsens and he goes to Lille to visit a specialist. On the way he encounters the Count's nephew on his motorcycle, returning for a while from the Foreign Legion. They have an intense conversation, and the priest is overjoyed to have met someone friendly and open to him—overjoyed as well to be treated to an experience like a motorcycle ride, the joy he thinks God has granted him so that he might experience the full pain and loss of death (figure 2.4). In Lille he learns that he has terminal stomach cancer.

8. This is the beginning of quite a persistent theme in his later films. Suicide is an issue in *Pickpocket*, *Au hasard, Balthazar*, *Mouchette*, *Une femme douce*, *The Devil, Probably*, and *L'Argent*.

While in the city, he enters a church, but feels no resonance and leaves without praying. He then visits an old friend from the seminary, Dufrety, who has left the priesthood and now lives with a woman out of wedlock. During the night, the priest's condition worsens, and he asks Dufrety for the last rites. His friend demurs since he is no longer a priest, but the priest responds with a line that has formed the basis for the bulk of the commentary on Bresson. "What does it matter? All is grace."

While there are all of these other characters in the film, we get no sense of their point of view, or no sense other than what the priest can register as another's point of view. So, most of what we learn about them is from visual evidence. As befits the trope of a visualized diary, the soul of the priest suffuses everything *he says we see*, but not necessarily what we see. In his engagement with the world we get an indirect view of that world: one that is not only without faith, but largely without serious meaningfulness; petty, small-minded, selfish, self-centered. Given the pure subjectivity of the film, we have to say we get the *priest's* sense of the world of the villagers, but from the dialogue and actions we have enough evidence to realize that he is not fantasizing or fabulating. Ambricourt is a miserable place. We "see" in the film how Bernanos sums up the place at the very opening of the diary, but the explicit recounting in the novel of the priest's impression is important.

> Mine is a parish like all the rest. They're all alike. Those of to-day, I mean . . .
>
> My parish is bored stiff; no other word for it. Like so many others! We can see them being eaten up by boredom, and we can't do anything about it. Some day perhaps we shall catch it ourselves—become aware of the cancerous growth within us. You can keep going a long time with that in you.[9]

This will be important to us later because it calls to mind an account by Heidegger of the disclosive significance of deep boredom. In a 1929–30 lecture source he notes, and we'll see the significance of this later: "This is why we asked whether perhaps contemporary man has become bored with himself, and whether a profound boredom is a fundamental attunement of contemporary Dasein."[10]

Bresson's film is only indirectly "about" a man with a deep religious faith; it is rather the expression of such a man's experiences. The film is about him only insofar as *he* is "about him." As such it is the record of a commitment

9. Bernanos (2002), 1. I think we should take quite seriously "Those of to-day, I mean . . ."

10. Heidegger (2000), 77.

and an implicit reflection by him on the meaning of commitment, what sustains it, what weakens it, the same theme pursued in *Angels of Sin*, *A Man Escaped*, *Pickpocket*, *The Trial of Joan of Arc*, and *Lancelot du Lac*. However, in the initial and much of the subsequent commentary on the film, a consensus of sorts has emerged that the film is the presentation of the life and sufferings of a saint, that Bresson means for us to take him as an actual saint, not just one in the priest's own mind. I noted earlier the apparent allusions to a suffering Son of God, and besides the bread and wine, there are several more. Bazin notes that the film does not really narrate a story; there is no character development, and, apart from the Countess, no character reversals. He notes that the film moves forward more like a medieval passion play or, even better, the stations of the cross. The priest even stumbles once in the mud, and his face is cleaned by Séraphita, in a Veronica's veil moment. He dies "between" two social outcasts on his own Golgotha. The priest even considers himself (the most important reference to how he thinks of himself) a "prisoner of His [Jesus's] Sacred Passion."[11] He welcomes his death as a "sacrifice." Indeed, the religious sensibility manifest in the diary appears to be Jansenist. As Durgnat puts it, "It is essential to the film, as to the novel, that the priest's suffering be maximal, his 'joy' obliterated, that he reach the limits of experience."[12] Goodness is unachievable in this world; there is only evil. The priest, the saint, has staked everything on the afterlife, God's justice, and so represents a kind of Christian tragic hero, made possible and finally redeemed in his bravery and sacrifice only by the gift of grace. Hence Bazin's remarks that the film is a "phenomenology of salvation and grace."[13]

There is something to all this; the priest's religiosity is at the center of everything in the film. But the emphasis on the priest's faith does not necessarily lead to the conclusion that the *film's* point of view is a sympathetic portrayal of heroic faith in the face of such indifference and in spite of such intense personal self-doubt. Consider these telling remarks by Bazin in discussing the crucial scene between the Countess and the priest: "The words themselves are so much dead weight, the echo of a silence that is the true dialogue between these two souls." In the film as a whole though, this is not true. *What* is said is quite important because it focuses our attention on a

11. Pipolo (2010) claims that the book is a "chronicle of a life lived in imitation of Christ," and that its chronicle "defines, in whatever terms it is humanly possible to comprehend, what it might mean to be a saint" (72). I agree that the film is a chronicle of a man *who thinks of himself that way*, but that is far from making "the film" the subject of such sentences.

12. Durgnat (1999) 50.

13. Bazin (1998), 34.

theme that is consistently "said" throughout the film, in response to which faith is only one option, and a faith like the priest's comes at a severe and costly price: a fragility and agonizing self-doubt, occasionally resolvable only by that unpredictable "gift," grace. That explicit and often mentioned theme in the film is, repeatedly, *justice*, much more so than faith or grace. I am not aware of any interpretation that notes the prominence of this topic. This is very likely because there are very few close readings of the details of Bresson's films. The fascination with his style and the atmospheric effects of that style, and the prominence of easy, sweeping generalizations about his religiosity, together with just as easy a reliance on the themes of Bernanos's novel as something just "repeated" or embodied in the film, foreclose such attention.

Consider the extraordinary repetition of the theme and its centrality in the crucial scenes, with Delbende, with Chantal in the confessional, with the Countess, and with the Count's nephew, Olivier, at the end, as well as in several minor scenes. The farmer Fabergas complains because he thinks he is being unfairly charged for a curtain-like shroud that covers the church entrance during his wife's funeral, and he complains that the church financially exploits the poor, that he shouldn't be charged. ("It's only just.") Louise the governess complains that she is being treated unfairly by Chantal. (More unfairly than the priest appears to realize. From what we have seen of them and the Count we can hardly call theirs a love affair. The Count is a serial womanizer and has no doubt used his position of power to coerce the penniless Louise.)[14] Chantal complains about the unfairness of the Count's plans to send her away to boarding school so he can carry on the affair unimpeded. The priest from Torcy tells him to keep order even though it is futile, that disorder always returns, that "the night undoes the work of the day." In a critical scene with Dr. Delbende, the priest is told that the two of them belong to "the same race";[15] the race that "holds on" no matter what; "why? no one knows." The key feature of this race is that they do not expect "justice." ("Injustice? I'm not one to go on about justice.") The motto of this race is "face facts" (*faire face*)—the crucial fact being there is no justice (and hence for the doctor, no God). Chantal tells him she does not want to confess or repent; all she wants is "justice." The Countess is full of hatred for a God that could have taken her young boy, rage at the injustice of such a fate. The priest realizes that he has no effective counterargument for this,

14. We never see her remotely happy or at peace, and we do see her weeping when she kneels in church.

15. This is the first of two times in the film when he is invited into a community. The second is even more important, when he is told by the Count's nephew that he is "one of them," has the same attitude as the Foreign Legion soldiers.

and says "I looked like a guilty man trying in vain to justify himself." Chantal overhears the conversation but unjustly spreads the word that the priest has tormented and in effect killed her mother (who dies the night of their spiritual battle) and so she triumphs. Louise is sent away, and the priest's relations with the Count's family are ruined forever. Chantal's cousin, home on leave from the legion, tells the priest they could have been friends, that the priest is like a legionnaire who does not believe life is worth living and that even God for these happy few stands for a justice they hate, a justice without honor. (He presumably means the injunction to love one's enemies.) Even the heroic priest complains with some bitterness at the end of the film about the injustice of the fact that he is dying of a disease that rarely strikes someone his age, and he says he is "ashamed" to go home with cancer, as if it were a judgment on him.

These scenes suggest, I want to show, that the substance of the film is not only an affirmation of how the priest's faith allows him to accept an unjust world. It is also an exploration of the nature of such injustice itself, the near universal sense among the characters that life itself is nothing but injustice, and whether we can expect ourselves to endure it, at least those of us without the "childlike" nature of the priest. Put another way, does the priest really understand what he is accepting, enduring, sacrificing himself for?

The priest from Torcy and Dr. Delbende are old friends, and when the young priest consults Delbende about his worsening condition, they have their one conversation in the film as the doctor palpates his stomach. Aside from what was summarized earlier, we can note that he is immediately sympathetic to the priest and encourages him to come see him if he wants to talk. He tells him he likes his eyes, the eyes of a faithful dog, not an entirely complimentary remark. (In order to be faithful, must one have the temperament of a dog?) Somehow, Delbende infers from feeling his stomach that he has inherited a condition due to "what was drunk before him." If he feels the tumor growing inside, he says nothing about it, except perhaps in noting that he is "not up to much" and that that it is too late to do anything for him. The priest compliments himself on his ability to detect the voice of a wounded soul.

Since Delbende's death, his probable suicide, affects the priest a great deal, the way the death is understood by the priest from Torcy later, at the funeral, tells us a great deal both about the Torcy priest and the status of the "wound" the doctor may have suffered. When, after the funeral, the priest hints to his older colleague about a possible suicide, the Torcy priest admits that Delbende was distraught about the collapse of his practice, that he believed to the end that his patients—especially the paying ones—would return, would ignore the rumors that he knew nothing about antiseptic

FIGURE 2.5

practices. But they never did return. However, his old friend claims, the truth is that the doctor had lost his faith and could not get over not believing. This however must be an interpretation, not a report; it is what the Torcy priest believes must happen when anyone "loses" their faith, as if Delbende could have survived the end of his practice had he had faith. There is no evidence of this. We have ourselves seen that, while Delbende has lost his faith, he was not in agony about the fact, had come to expect nothing in the world but injustice. (The Torcy priest never suggests that the death was the result of an accidental discharge of the gun, apparently the official cause of death.) The priest is devastated by this, and says these words were like molten lead poured into an open wound (figure 2.5). (He is no doubt thinking of the danger he has experienced, were he to lose his faith, as he thinks he might.)

The young priest then indicates a worry that a suicide forecloses the possibility of salvation, and the Torcy priest interrupts him, and raises the justice theme again, claiming that Delbende was a just man and God is the God of the just. But again, Delbende, like everyone we have seen in the village with the exception of the Countess, either thinks that the situation they find themselves in is unjust (in the case of Delbende, universally unjust) or are indifferent to the issue. Cinematically or atmospherically, Bresson has portrayed life in the village as suspicious, greedy, small-minded, and without any common orientation of any significance. When the Torcy priest then says, oddly, that "we are at war and must fight the enemy," he appears to be admitting that *whatever the truth*, we must find a way to believe in a just order of a universe ruled by a loving God, "or Satan wins" (or at least we must find a way to convince others of this, no matter what we believe). If we don't manage to get ourselves to believe this, we might suffer the same fate as Delbende, painful words for the wavering curé. (The Torcy priest may be jaded and the representative of cautious conventionalism, but he reminds us of his own original religiosity when he is later so moved by the priest's purity that he asks for his blessing, instead of giving him his.)

And while it may be true for villagers in the 1930s that faith in such justice *could* be a main source of meaningfulness—that is, what matters above all, the horizon within which anything can matter or be endured—such sources of mattering are not subject to human control, as if a strategy in a war. Perhaps a hundred years earlier, they had been. But something has happened, something historical that Bresson will pursue with more and more explicitness. This is the deeper and more general issue than the appeal to grace reveals. We see the priest in despair over divine silence, and we then see him recovered. But he has not convinced himself to recover, argued himself into it; no one has helped him recover. (We can see, though, how desperate he would be if he could not convince himself that his faith had returned.) What comes to matter to us or not is subject to such contingency (a.k.a. grace) that our existential burden is to endure such a fate, come to understand what a life could be if this is the burden to be endured, especially, in contrast to the priest, to endure the finality of death. This is something that makes the reception of any such "gift" constantly insecure. We can even work to realize what we believe ought to matter, even if we know that that end does not subjectively matter to us; we are acting in this manner because we find that *beliefs* about what ought to matter have come to matter a great deal (and that is a rare event in itself, despite what people may tell themselves). The situation can become so extreme that we can find (and find or discover is the right word, not determine or decide) that very little, if anything, deeply matters to us, matters enough to be a source of significance in a life project, and one could say that for Bernanos and Heidegger and Bresson the result is boredom, a disclosive *Stimmung* or attunement for Heidegger because it discloses our sense of the paucity of available sources of mattering, a failure of general significance, something Heidegger and, I want to show, Bresson consider uniquely typical of later modern Western life, not because of any general, inescapable sinfulness of human being. This means, especially for our priest, as he is finding, that the fate of personal faith in a generally faithless world (Ambricourt as a microcosm) is not a matter of individual strength or continual gifts from God. If it is to be sustainable or does not just require rare and uncertain and repeated and arbitrary "gifts" of grace, it must also find some collective resonance in the world, must make sense in a world at a time. There is no such resonance in Ambricourt, not a single sustaining ally for the priest, and so it is Ambricourt that is battering the priest's faith, or the condition of "injustice," the lack of any reliable moral order and so the proliferation of greed, self-serving, arrogance, vanity, a situation that will be more and more prominent in Bresson's films starting with *Pickpocket* and exploding in *Au hasard, Balthazar* and *Mouchette*.

The second scene in which this situation is prominent, baffling, and disturbing for the man of faith is his relationship with Chantal, the Count's daughter, and it comes to a head in the most beautifully photographed scene in the film, when Chantal comes to visit him in order to insist that he hurry up and intervene to prevent her from being sent away. There is a growing similarity in these scenes: the discussion about the meaning of Delbende's suicide; Chantal's visit to the church; the long, tense conversation with the Countess; and the somewhat jocular nihilism of Olivier, the Count's nephew. All follow very closely the dialogue from the novel, but by excising much else from Bernanos's context, and by focusing so much on Laydu's remarkable face, Bresson makes the loneliness of the priest much more visibly painful. Nowhere is that isolation and the hopelessness it creates more apparent than in his dealing with Chantal.

Chantal's appearance in the church, rather than the rectory, alarms the priest. He feels it is inappropriate, no doubt mindful of the Count, and this is expressive of his anxiety about the difference between personal and ministerial counseling. But before they can sort that out, he experiences her nearly uncontrollable rage at and hatred for Louise, her governess. When she later says that she does not want to confess anything, that all she is asking for is "justice," it is clear what she means. She feels betrayed, and she wants the betrayal rectified. She had trusted Louise, thought that she had kind eyes, but now (after learning of the affair and their plans to banish her from her family home) she would like "to tear out those eyes and crush them underfoot like nuts!" Her peroration ends with her insisting that she will either kill Louise or kill herself. Tellingly, the priest's first response is not moral or psychological but a warning: "Have you no fear of God?" The priest asks her to kneel in the confessional, but she refuses, and the scene is photographed with her looking down at the priest from out of darkness (figure 2.6).

FIGURE 2.6

The anger in Chantal continues to pour out of her. She hates her mother for not protecting her. "She's a fool and a coward." She lost respect for her father. She will go off and disgrace herself (one assumes, become pregnant), and that will redress the wrongs. But the priest has been paying attention earlier when Chantal had mentioned suicide, and he intuits that she has actually made plans. He suddenly asks for the suicide letter, no doubt accusatory, meant to injure her father, and she hands it over, amazed at his intuition, "You must be the devil." When the scene is over, the priest had written without elaboration in the diary, "I was nothing but a miserable, unworthy priest." His sense of his failure perhaps had something to do with the fact that he can only respond to Chantal's pain by threatening her with divine punishment if she does anything wrong: no sympathy, no comfort, no explanation of what he'll do for her in fulfillment of his promise to help. (He will mention to the Countess that they are banning her from her family home, but he does not have the nerve to say that to the Count, to whom he only mentions her fragile mental state. Our memory of his hesitancy and cowardice when confronted by the bar owner returns.) This response, by wide agreement the most important in the film, is significant because it sets the tone of the next episode, casts a shadow over the episode that I think has been undervalued by critics.

I mentioned when discussing the priest's crisis of faith that it is not entirely internal or psychological. His faith is his faith in both God and his vocation as a priest, and both require some reciprocal resonance, some sort of response, reflection back from outside one's own mental life. In the case of God, he hears mostly silence; when he thinks he hears someone calling for him and goes to the window he finds nothing but such silence. But not entirely; he feels reassured to some extent, at least heard, if not addressed. But the fact that his vocation to minister is rejected by the town is the deeper source of the crisis. The religious dimension of life he so values has no such resonance in Ambricourt, and that makes his faith almost impossible to sustain. But in this regard, he shares something interesting with Chantal.

In the complex web of daily meaningfulness, our investment in the affairs of the world could be put more strongly than our practical concerns, the requirements in ordinary daily life to get this or that done. Such stable meaningfulness is something we are implicitly thankful for; it inspires an erotic attachment to the world, a love that is only possible if somehow reciprocated. (This has a great deal to do with the theme of justice, as we have been seeing.) This is of course not so simple as the world "loving us back," but involves in some way feeling at home, secure in a web of meaningfulness, and that includes our investment in a primary source of meaningfulness from the beginning of life: the family. But that source of significance and any "return" acknowledgment can fail, break down, and it has, spectacularly, in Chantal's family. Chantal knows that she is not loved. Her mother sees her only as someone who will disturb her indifference, her ability to ignore her husband's infidelities. So, obsessed by the death of her son, the only thing that matters to her (certainly not Chantal) is her hatred of an unjust God. Her concern with Chantal is just to send her away. The Count, concerned only with his self-indulgence and his status, also wants her out of the picture. Louise, with whom Chantal had once felt close, sees her as a threat to her survival in the family, her only source of income.

So, it is not surprising that the priest has that moment of deep intuitive understanding of Chantal, understands, without knowing how or why he knows, the extraordinary depth of Chantal's rage and suicidal despair. We could say that he recognizes himself in Chantal, and this because they share this experience of the lack of resonance of what matters to them anywhere in the world they happen to find themselves—for the priest, Ambricourt; for Chantal, her family. Chantal's later contempt for the priest after her "victory" in having Louise sent away instead of her very likely reflects her anxiety and to some extent shame that she has been so well understood.

In the next scene, we yet again encounter someone whose love of the world has died, who finds nothing worth mattering and is consumed by rage about the absence of sustainable meaningfulness (again, a justice that makes sense), the Countess, played with extraordinary force by a veteran actress, unusual in the rest of Bresson's films, Rachel Bérendt. The priest begins this great struggle with the Countess by explaining that he is concerned with Chantal's mental health. When he mentions the possibility of suicide to the Countess, she responds with great coldness that "that is the last thing she'll do. She's terribly afraid of death." The Countess does not believe the priest could understand such things, given his age and limited experience, and she asks if he is afraid of death. He nods slightly in agreement. Fear, the first issue of salience that he raised with Chantal, returns, and ultimately forms the basis of his ability to reconcile the Countess to God. He says he fears death but less his death than hers, and we will see that he means if she dies not in the state of grace, hating God, she will be denied heaven and the chance to see her son again.

Throughout the scene, we intermittently hear the sound of someone raking leaves on a hard surface, typical of the use of sound in the film. Dogs barking are the most frequent off camera sounds, but cocks crowing, wheels creaking on pavements, wind, a stray gunshot are also heard. (One can also count silence for longer than any filmgoer would expect as another such "sound."[16]) They are all in effect "stray sounds," the kind of thing most film editors would edit out rather than deliberately include. They do not, in other words, accompany or intensify images (as they do in other films, like *A Man Escaped* or *Mouchette*).[17] Their randomness here creates an atmosphere of contingency, of life happening in various unconnected dimensions, within the context of which, in unpredictable ways, something suddenly and of great consequence can occur. A man is raking leaves while a struggle over a woman's soul is going on; a dog is barking as a young priest anxiously takes up his new parish, his life's vocation; someone whistling immediately suggests what will be the village's indifference to his arrival; we hear the sounds of a wheelbarrow's squeaking, and we see a huge barrel of wine for the priest, intimating the scope of his need; a priest hears a gunshot while riding his bike, and it will portend a crisis of faith. It is the kind of thing Barthes called a "punctum" in a photograph, and it contributes an intensification of the realism that belies any obvious authorial intention to create something realistic, as in merely ocular or social realism or by virtue of any camera automatism. This would be in the way a random detail in a novel, unconnected to anything in the plot, anchors us in reality in a way that extensive and detailed description of what

16. "The soundtrack invented silence." *NC* 28.
17. See Hanlon (1998).

is going on in the plot could not. In the case of this scene, the impression is of an indifferent world carrying on mundane tasks, while everything of any significance is at stake for the Countess. All of this intensifies the theme of some worldly resonance, and especially the lack of it.

They begin discussing Chantal, but as noted, the Countess quickly dismisses the priest's concerns, insisting both that Chantal is too afraid of death to harm herself and that, anyway, she, the Countess, doesn't care. She has had to get used to the Count's infidelities and his humiliation of her; let Chantal do the same. But the conversation changes dramatically when the priest suddenly says in response to this maternal coldness, "God will break you." When the Countess says that he has already broken her, meaning that he took her young son from her, the main issue is addressed. The priest's chief case to the Countess is stark: "The coldness of your heart may keep him [her dead son] from you forever." And the justice theme returns as the Countess responds that God does not take revenge, and that keeping her from her son is not just, it is madness. It is at this point that the priest, in a diary voice-over, facing the "imperious" Countess, confesses that he felt like a guilty man trying to justify himself, and perhaps that is just what he is. He seems to feel guilty because, as he confesses later, he has had moments of despair and some bitterness like the Countess, and he is trying to justify keeping faith with God even though he has his own doubts and he has no effective way to convince her either that the death of her son or divine punishment for her is "just." But a moment of visible illness in the priest, which the Countess notices as he appears ready to leave, breaks the tension and the conversation takes on a more urgent turn when the Countess, justifying her claim that such a punishment, keeping her from her son, would be unjust, says it is because "love is stronger than death." This is the only point where divine love is mentioned, as the priest responds somewhat moralistically first, that love has its own "order and rules," and later says that God proved his love by Jesus's sacrifice, that God is love itself. But he reverts to his main claim quickly, that she must resign herself to the fate God has ordained and that she has no idea what ill effects her bitter thoughts can have in this world. Indeed, he says that if God gave us a clear idea of how bound we are together in good and evil (that evil is unavoidable, inevitable, no matter the good we sometimes do) we could not live. He says this even though he has just admitted that we do have such an idea; he has just insisted on it. She continues to say that she hates God, that he has ceased to matter to her, and that turns out to be the pivot of their struggle: the priest says that in such extremity she is now "face to face" with God in admitting her hatred, and this moves her. She sits, somewhat crestfallen, and clutches the locket with a picture of her son but continues to insist she would do anything to be free of God, no matter the costs (figure 2.7).

FIGURE 2.7

But when the priest admits that he has felt exactly the same way (the image of Delbende appears before his eyes and he must mean the credibility of Delbende's loss of faith), it appears to move her again. Continuing his somewhat inconsistent form of reasoning, he insists that she cannot bargain with God at the same time as he promises that if she yields, she will be rewarded with the prospect of seeing her son again. Now she asks what she must say, balks again at "thy will be done," but again he promises her reunion, repeats the bargain he has denied offering. At this point she is indeed "broken." She says that now she has nothing, that her life meant something when it was so focused on the injustice of God, but the priest now says, "Give Him everything," and she throws the locket into the fire. He hurriedly retrieves it, tells her that God is no torturer; she kneels, and he touches her bowed head and blesses her (figure 2.8).

Since philosophical attention first focused on the notion of justice (*dike*) the basic intuitive understanding of it has been what Heidegger called "fittingness."[18] Not merely the redress of wrongs, or compensation, or desert, or fairness, or what is due one (as in Plato's *Republic*'s case for each person

18. This is a loose translation of "Fug" as Heidegger uses it in *The Introduction to Metaphysics* (2000), 171, a word connected to joint, connection, arrangement.

FIGURE 2.8

doing the job he is most suited for), although all of those are relevant, but something much more comprehensive—a way of living "fittingly," as befits a being whose own being is at issue for it in a world suitable for such a being, a being with the capacity to interrogate the possibility of meaningful existence or world at all, and so in a human world "befitting," open to, responsive to, such a being. In the Western tradition the primary source of such meaningfulness and so a "fitting" life has been taken to be reason in a broad sense, that is, not just reason in the sense of justification (why should this have happened and not that, or why should this have happened to me and not to her) but in the general sense of intelligibility (as in: I understand the child's death because I understand what disease killed him and how it did. In that sense, it makes sense). Indeed, since the original Greek speculation, the world's goodness, its suitability for the beings we are (open to interrogation) and our suitability for it (our being rational), depends on this compatibility, that the questions we ask of the world can be, at least in principle, answered. It is on such a basis that we can be said to be at home in the world. We demand that the world make sense in that register (rationally, as in the Principle of Sufficient Reason, that nothing can happen without a sufficient reason for it happening) and the world's responsiveness to such a demand is what makes the "fitting" life, living justly, as one ought, possible.

It does not take a long digression into Heidegger to suggest that there is something deeply insufficient, even dogmatic and arbitrary, about such a way of looking at sense and sense making. Of course, it would be absurd and intolerable if the laws of physics sometimes applied and sometimes did not, if some people with identical bodies lived for ten and others for a thousand years, but looking at things that way is of no use to the Countess. She is asking for an account that makes sense in a way not addressed by explanation alone, or at least not by rational explanation alone.[19] Her anguish is caused by her prior assumption that the world is governed by a purposeful and benevolent intelligence, and so that what matters in human life, like love, must have a place in a purposeful and good world, that such matters are in that sense supported by the world. It is not "just," fitting, if the families on which we all so totally depend are scenes of competition, jealousy, vanity, exploitation, and manipulation; nor is it just if the overwhelming love for our children that we are so powerfully inclined to is "answered" by arbitrary and purposeless death. It is in this context that the priest's "case" to the Countess remains within the rational tradition: it will all *ultimately* make sense, have a reason. God will reward the just and faithful and punish the unjust or unfaithful; whatever might seem unjust in existence, like the death of a small, beloved child, will be compensated for (for the faithful) by eternal life together. Despite what he says he is doing, the priest has actually bullied the Countess into submission by threatening her with the alternative—eternal separation from her son. He has in fact pushed a bargain on her, not revived any genuine faith. (Chantal has given everyone a distorted version of what she saw,[20] but the priest's role in "breaking" the Countess, and the later charge of "blackmail" by the Torcy priest, mean that what Chantal has said is not totally unfair.) Of course, once the Countess has come to believe in such a compensation, her whole perspective changes, and she joyously anticipates her death, which comes quickly. (She sends a note thanking the priest, whom she calls "another child," says she is not merely resigned, but happy, that she does not know how it happened but has stopped asking and is at peace.) But this all still is based on a narrow, not a broad and deep conception of justice. It means that there is only one sort of directedness that is just or fitting in a human life

19. In the Socratic tradition and its aftermath, the kinds of questions the Countess is asking are not addressed. They are pertinent to Greek tragic poetry, but these are tragedies just because there is no logos, no answer to her questions. That is not acceptable to philosophy, as one can see from Kant's antipathy to tragedy and in the efforts of philosophers to domesticate tragedy. See Pippin (2021b), 19–38.

20. It was the Countess on her own who threw the medallion into the fire; the priest did not demand she do that.

in the world in which we find ourselves: keeping this sort of bargain; faithfulness and endurance of the arbitrary in this life, in the hope of eternal compensation and peace. And finding meaning in such a directedness, even at that calculative level, or even at a more full-throated and joyous embrace of God's mysterious ways, is something possible, we say, and the film seems to affirm, by means of grace, a gift. That is just as arbitrary as the original son's death. God may "break" the Countess's hard heart, but there is no sense (no justice) in the fact that if the priest had not stopped by that day, if he had not been the occasion for this gift, she would have died with the same deep hatred of God she had lived with for years.

Now this might seem unfairly abstract, this way of noting that for the priest, for Delbende, for Chantal, and for the Countess, some basic relation to the world, an absorption in, care for, sense of meaningful place in, the world, has been broken, and they are looking for some way back. (It may not be how Bernanos would put it, whose sensibility does seem Jansenist, on the same side as the priest's.) But the film shows us other dimensions. I say too abstract or framed in too philosophical a way since the religious approach, and basically one dimension of a religious approach—keeping faith—is so prominent in the film. But prominent does not mean affirmed, and in each of the scenes where the priest intervenes (or in his own case) however much his "diary subjectivity" suffuses the atmosphere created cinematically, there are still internal tensions in the point of view that he is unaware of. There is no denying the integrity and purity of the priest's commitment. The limitations have to do with his general unworldliness, lack of self-awareness, or what is several times noted as his childishness, all of which can be captured by the camera much more clearly than in Bernanos's prose.[21] (His relationship with Séraphita is constant confirmation of this. He is so easily mocked and tricked by a mere "mean girl," so often so confused and hurt by a bullying adolescent that one feels for him the way one would feel for a boy in her class.) In general, the absence of vice is not virtue, but innocence. Virtue is the struggle with and overcoming of vice. The priest struggles of course to keep faith, but his struggle is with himself, not with "temptation" to selfishness or avarice or vanity. (Imagine how different a film if he were shown to be attracted to Chantal.) And he does not seem to understand how hopeless (or how endless) his attempts to reassure himself about himself are. This is why the closing scene with Olivier is so important, since he begins to see what any sort of life other than the sheltered one that has been his fate would be, and he tries to come to terms

21. One recalls again the emphasis, for Séraphita and for Delbende, on his eyes, his faithful, doglike eyes.

FIGURE 2.9

with the fact that such an option opens up to him just as it is closed down by the gravity of his illness, a final injustice if ever there was. There is thus a great pathos in the long shot of the isolated priest running toward the manor upon hearing of the Countess's death, as if he is needed there, wholly ignored by the Count, surprised that there is not a smile on the Countess's face (figure 2.9).

And it is certainly worth noting that the occasion of the Countess's conversion, or reversion to faith, is for the priest no confirmation of his own faith. He says to himself, "What wonder that one can give what one does not possess. O miracle of empty hands." It is extraordinary that at this moment, the only real success in his ministry at the village, there is no comfort or consolation in the success. He has given the Countess peace of mind and faith in the afterlife, but he has none himself. We will need to remember this when we consider the famous closing scenes of the film.

Despite his hesitancy and humility, it is certainly still possible to associate what the priest had been doing with self-sacrifice. He refuses to defend himself with the canon, endures the humiliation he receives from the villagers,[22] refuses to show the letter he received (perhaps all an echo of Jesus's confrontation with Pilate), and so it is possible to see him as many have, despite his

22. He can be compared to Balthazar in this respect.

FIGURE 2.10

naivete and childlike lack of self-awareness, as a Christ figure. Even his self-doubt might call to mind Christ's last words on the cross, his feeling that he has been forsaken. He certainly sees *himself* that way in his last conversation with his mentor from Torcy. He says that "he always returns to the olive grove," Christ's torment in Gethsemane, and that he now realizes through the gift of the Lord's grace that he was a prisoner of the "Holy Agony," secure in his place in eternity. This all seems highly improbable since a major trope in the film, if not the major one, is the priest's ill health, which obviously has nothing to do with Jesus.[23] There is a cancer eating away at him, a constitutional weakness, doubt, and confusion, debilitating him more every day, leaving him less and less able to withstand the profane and petty world of the village.

Those looking for confirmation of such a Christ association however might still point to his last contact with Séraphita. He has visited several parishioners and falls ill on the way home, falling face down into the mud. (We learn from Séraphita, who finds him on the road, that he has probably been slipped something by one of the villagers because they would find doing so amusing; figure 2.10.)

23. Apart from the fact that he seems to be starving himself, deluding himself about what he can and cannot eat, in an attempt to identify himself with Jesus's sacrifice, an identification that borders on vanity.

FIGURE 2.11

Séraphita, as the priest once remarked, is unusually "mature," and in this scene she assumes a maternal role, cleaning his face and explaining what the villagers have likely done to him, leading him back to the road. This further emphasizes his childishness, especially now in contrast with Séraphita's worldliness and psychological sophistication. But her unremitting hostility to him has clearly been broken by her experience of his weakness and suffering, and this does seem to be a case where the priest's willingness to sacrifice himself, his purity of purpose and integrity, has a dramatic effect on the cynical girl, all of which is captured in the simple beauty of his being led by the hand of a child. While there is nothing transcendent or religious about Chantal's change, it is a moment of humanity and tenderness rare in the film (figure 2.11).

The severity of the priest's illness convinces him that he must see a specialist in Lille, and as he sets off for the train station, he meets the dashing and charming Olivier, the Count's nephew, on his motorcycle.

We have already remarked on the priest's acceptance of what he experiences as an injustice: that he has been allowed to feel like a young man open to adventure, risk, happiness, and friendship just at the moment of his dying so that his sacrifice would be as thorough (and devastating) as possible. But Olivier's very unusual claim is that he, a soldier with martial virtues and an indifference to death, and the priest share a bond, could have been friends. That is, raising again the priest's unknowingness, he says that the priest could appreciate this if he could see himself, clearly implying that he can't. This, their bond, is an even stranger thing to say to the priest, because he goes on to say that the soldiers know that God has no involvement with the world, that he will not save them, and so they have no use for him, prefer "all or nothing," the risk of life for the sake of honor and glory. "Admit it," he says, "our world is not theirs." (He means the ordinary world, the world of convention and conformity, the world summarized by a character in *Au hasard, Balthazar* as "I love money, and I hate death.") In Olivier's version of their world, God stands for the promise of a justice they despise, a justice without honor. He appears to sense in the priest a kindred feeling that the idea of a world suffused with God's love, or a world that offers credible sources of meaningfulness, is a delusion; there is only injustice or a justice without honor, which might describe the stance of faith. The priest is clearly upset and confused, but the train arrives before he can respond.

After he receives his diagnosis of terminal stomach cancer from the specialist in Lille, the priest enters an old church but reports that he had never felt such a "physical revulsion to prayer," the culmination in a way of his great difficulty in praying throughout his diary. (Given the absence of any real presence of God or indications of what so many commentators call manifestations of "transcendence" in Bresson's depiction, what would be the point?) His will, he writes, is helpless in the face of this revulsion, and he turns and leaves the church. He had earlier wondered if praying to be able to pray counted as prayer, but even that now seems pointless. Perhaps this is why Olivier had seen a bond between them. There is clearly no just God who might intervene to redress the injustice of a young priest dying at the beginning of his life, at least no God who might be responsive to prayer.

He then makes his way to the apartment of a friend from his seminary days, Dufrety, who had taken a leave from the ministry because of illness. He is another "twin" of the priest, emaciated, ill: both youths with "rotten blood in their veins," which he attributes to their being "intellectuals" and so undernourished. Dufrety is a bit of a boastful windbag, talking aimlessly without noticing how much the priest is suffering and near collapse (figure 2.12). Finally the priest does collapse, and when he awakens, pleads that he doesn't want to die there. The woman with whom Dufrety lives tends to him and explains that she has devoted herself to Dufrety but will not marry him because she wants to leave it open to him to start religious life anew when and if he ever gets well.

FIGURE 2.12

The priest falls more and more gravely ill, and we see the letter that Dufrety has written to the Torcy priest, describing the priest's last, dying moments. As we hear the account, for almost two minutes, all we see is the black cross, not a crucifix, just a mysterious black cross (figure 2.13).

The priest asks Dufrety for absolution, which of course he cannot officially grant because he is not ordained. The priest's last words are "What does it matter? All is grace." Strictly speaking, and in accordance with his vocation, absolution, a final confession, the last rites ("extreme unction") are fundamentally important. It would ensure that one dies in a state of grace and will be admitted to heaven. And while there is a great deal of attention to the priest's invocation of grace, there has not been much attention to the priest's final indifference to what should be a crucial component of his clerical role; his own ministry to the dying is supposed to matter. If absolution does not matter, what would it mean to be a priest? What matters is grace, a gift of faith, something one cannot achieve, predict, count on, resolve to have, or even ask or pray for. This suggests a world indifferent to human concerns, unable in human experience to offer up any stable source of purpose or significance except contingently, even arbitrarily. Consequently, that final image of the plain black cross embodies the duality inherent in the priest's last two sentences. It is, on

FIGURE 2.13

the one hand, testimony to his faith; on the other hand, in its opacity and mysteriousness, it is terrifying. I don't think Bresson means us to think of this as an implication of the human condition as such, but one consequent to a distinctive human world that has lost any source of orienting significance, something that becomes more and more explicit in his later films. That is what I want to show in what follows.

3
Atmosphere as World in *Pickpocket*

The notion of a human world as understood by philosophers like Martin Heidegger is not the totality of all that is the case. It is best understood as a horizon of possible meaningfulness in our engagements with objects, nature, and other human beings. All such beings are originally or "primordially" available in experience in varying degrees of significance. Our perceptual and cognitive capacities are obviously in play, but the thought is that we do not originally experience objects as, say, rectangular, solid, colored, reflecting light, but as desks, or as tools, signs of rain, friends, strangers, threats, holy, negligible, or mysterious. Such encounters can only occur in a shared context of significance that is not itself a possible object of experience since such a context is an always already assumed condition of all such experience. So, our sense of being in such a world, always a historical world (like "the early Christian world" or "the modern Western world") is necessarily indirect, never an "object" for a "subject." As Heidegger puts it, we find ourselves "attuned" to such scales of significance, significances that are disclosed rather than projected. These are claims about, very roughly, the role of contextuality and our sensitivity to background context in the possibility of meaning—that have been made by many other anti-Cartesian philosophers. But what distinguishes Heidegger's approach is his claim about the primordial and the secondary, and his treatment of the former as an ontological issue, as one that concerns the meaning of being itself.

But how might one *film* such a contextual condition, bring it to light on film? The claim here is that one of the great achievements of Bresson's films is to have achieved a way of "showing" such worldliness by unusual cinematic techniques that create a background atmosphere or tonality, rigorously controlled in the films, that suggest ways in which such a world of possible significances, the original ways in which beings show up as mattering (or as failing to matter), might be understood, made present to the viewer. The films provide a nondiscursive modality of the intelligibility of worldliness by the control of such an atmospheric presence, something very like what Heidegger means by attunement. My example in this chapter is his 1959 film *Pickpocket*.

Pickpocket is often chosen by cineasts as his most quintessentially typical film.[1] All the major stylistic elements that make his films so instantly recognizable are present in uncompromising force. The supervening intention is clearly, as always, to avoid treating cinema as filmed theater: no professional actors and no real acting; hence minimal expressivity and a de-psychologization of the presentation of character, sometimes to an almost automaton level; little if any reference to characters' intentions as explanations of actions, and indeed little evidence of reflective self-awareness. What little evidence there is, like Michel's (Martin LaSalle) writing in what appears to be a diary, is mysterious and untrustworthy. Although the film turns into an exploration of Michel's state of mind, his motivation, his self-justification, his sense of his place in the world, and his relation to those close to him, this is all, in effect, a task transferred to the viewer and the viewer's inferential powers, powers that require sensitivity to the atmosphere or mood of the film mentioned above. As we shall see, the atmospheric effect of Bresson's minimalism is another feature of his style that is not motivated only by cinematic purity. That atmosphere is suffused with an arid lifelessness, an existential deadness in which anything one can do that can create an erotic (or any other kind of) frisson, life, energy, danger, thrill, is shown to be irresistible. For most of the film, Michel's expression varies very little. Even what must be for him the most traumatic event in the film, the death of his mother and the self-assessment it must occasion, seems just to pass through him with little turbulence. We are asked to make sense of what we are seeing—an educated young man's turn to crime and the development of his relation with a young woman—with all the usual expressive clues about mindedness kept to a bare minimum. There is a kind of test for whether we have understood him and what about him we have understood in the last scene of the film, as is so often the case in Bresson's films. I want to suggest that we have understood a great deal despite the inadequacy of the psychological concepts we are forced to use. We understand him by having become

1. For example, Benoît Jacquot, cited in Semoulé (1993), 87. In 1965, *Cahiers du Cinéma* pronounced *Pickpocket* the most important film of the 1945–65 period. See Sémoulé, 18.

more attuned to his being in a world, a world available only atmospherically. As we shall see, Michel is no raging nihilist, but he inhabits a world that fails to inspire any concerned investment, even the investment of love. Whether he finds a way to reengage with life in such a world, or even finds love, is the question raised by the last scene.

There are many other typical Bressonian touches. Minimal mise-en-scène. A de-emphasis on plot continuity in favor of ellipses. Minimal use of music; in this case one moment from Louis XIV's musical director Jean-Baptiste Lully's opera *Atys* repeated a few times and never to guide or manipulate emotion. Unconventional, quite minimal scene staging, with the stationary camera often lingering on empty spaces, stairwells, open doors. And as in these other films, the questions raised by the unconventional formal stylistic innovations are about how Bresson thinks we come to "understand" what we are seeing, in what ways the film can be said to register on, make some sort of impression on us. It is easy enough to follow the plot, understand the characters' minimal accounts of themselves to each other, but we are also being invited to consider what sense Michel's life, his mode of being, makes to him. And, as with other films, the question of making some sense of Michel and his fate must include the context, the sociohistorical postwar Parisian world that includes Jeanne and her fate (abandoned by her parents, abandoned by the father of her child), Michel's mother (stolen from by, and practically abandoned by, her son), Jacques (a moralist with no morals), Kassagi (the expert mentor in pickpocketing), and the Inspector (playing some sort of odd game with Michel). (He is once said to have "evil" eyes—"*malin*," cunning, malicious.)[2] We come to wonder what there is about that world that seems to have no place in it for Michel, or at least no place he can find. (What we know of the world Michel is trying to find a place in is as minimal as what the film discloses about him.) Minimality increases intensity.

There are also several framing devices, ways of setting what would appear to be context for understanding the general point of the film. *Pickpocket* tells the story of an aspiring writer (who apparently has written nothing),[3] Michel, who, without explanation, goes to the Longchamp

2. "Le malin" is a euphemism for the devil.

3. Except for the written recollections we hear voiced four times in the film, reprising the technique Bresson had used in *Diary*, although in that film the writing was present not past tense, a diary not a memoir or autobiography. In many ways, Michel is a kind of counterpart curé, as dedicated, but to crime. The suspicion of self-deception is also a similarity.

racecourse one day and tries to become a pickpocket.[4] He is immediately arrested. (A major ellipsis already: we don't see the arrest or learn why he was suspected. There is no conversation in the car as he sits between two detectives. He has a wad of money on him but somewhat mysteriously—given that there must have been some evidence that he stole the money—he is released.) He eventually gets pretty good at his new craft and joins a gang of such thieves. We learn, in the sketchiest of ways, that he is someone who believes that his superiority (superiority in what is never explained) puts him above the law. He is investigated by an unusually kind and thoughtful Inspector who finally catches him, and he appears unrepentant and still convinced of his superman theory until, at the last moment, in the final scene in the film when he is in prison, he suddenly appears to be willing to reenter the human and humane world when he (apparently)[5] experiences the selfless love of a young woman.

Obviously, Dostoyevsky's *Crime and Punishment* is a "source" of the film, is meant to be one of those major framing devices. But what could "source" mean here? These elements alone clearly show it as a reference point that a literate viewer would recognize. There are even more direct references, despite the broad changes in the narrative. Michel is a struggling writer not a student, but he lives in a garret like Raskolnikov and hides his money in a baseboard. He is strangely indifferent to money and seems much more intrigued by the craft of pickpocketing and his main motivation, if it can even be called that, seems to be simply to get better at it. His clownish, ill-fitting suit is mentioned twice but even after his success at crime, he does not buy a new one, as he is advised to. This is emphasized to the point of comedy. At one point we are told that he leaves Paris for two years, and when he returns, he returns to exactly the spot in the train station from which he departed and in exactly the same ridiculous ill-fitting suit, exactly the same shirt and tie. There is a dialogue at one point very similar to Porfiry Petrovich's revelation to Raskolnikov that he knows who the murderer is and that it "is you!" The film Inspector mimics such a revelation about Michel's worst crime—stealing from his ill mother. Jeanne tells Michel that he is not interested in the things that interest others, almost literally what the fiancé of Raskolnikov's sister tells him. And there are other parallels between

4. We learn later that Michel has stolen money from his mother, producing a shame so great that he cannot face her, even as her illness worsens. When he gives Jeanne money to give to his mother, it seems, in that context, like a restitution, and we might assume he feels himself driven to crime so that he can pay back his mother.

5. Apparently because, as we shall see, Jeanne never expresses any love for Michel, and when he asks her why she comes to visit him, she says honestly, "You're all I've got."

Jeanne and Sonya, Jacques and Razumikin, Raskolnikov's friend. In both cases, the kindly detective is trying to convince the criminal to confess, at least a possible step toward repentance and reform. But in *Pickpocket*, we have every indication that the Inspector has all the evidence he needs to arrest Michel from the very beginning. He releases him without explanation, lets him know that he knows that Michel is guilty but does nothing, even arrests the two other members of his gang, with whom he has been constantly working, but does not arrest Michel. And Michel never does confess,[6] much less repent.

But once we notice the reference, we realize how diminished in seriousness the frame story of the film is. The brutal axe murder of an old woman and her sister has here become pickpocketing, a diminishment that seems almost bathetic. A superior man should be allowed to get away with . . . pickpocketing? There is something faintly comic about the crime itself, in the way sleight-of-hand magic tricks inspire laughter, and in the way the clueless victim is "magically" relieved of his money.[7] Moreover, Bresson makes it hard to think of Michel's crimes as crimes rather than tricks, because he never shows us the consequences of the crimes for the victim, instead creating the impression that they all have more money than they need. Raskolnikov's tortured psychological musings, his obsession with his guilt, are gone. (Michel never expresses any guilt whatsoever about his pickpocketing, only about his theft from his mother.) In the place of Raskolnikov's fevered reflections, we have this thoroughly unreflective, somewhat whiny, self-pitying, petulant man. There is no reference to religion in what appears to be his conversion at the end, as there is, albeit ambiguously, in *Crime and Punishment*. The Michel-Raskolnikov connection is certainly deliberate, but there is very little genuinely Raskolnikovian about Michel. It is hard to imagine Michel subject to Raskolnikov's fainting spells, or his four days of feverish, guilt-induced delirium. This makes us suspect that a prideful self-delusion, a need for status and importance that, we might infer, are difficult to achieve in this society, are much more prominent than Raskolnikov's attempts to justify his murder. We learn something of the state of Michel's soul, typically in Bresson, not from his own reflections, musings, or words, but much more indirectly, by having Dostoyevsky called to mind, and when in mind, by ironicizing Michel's pretensions. Michel's pettiness, by contrast, seems at home in the daily pettiness of his world, just

6. He tells Jeanne a confession was made, but just in order to withdraw it later and complicate his prosecution.

7. Kassagi, whose criminal career was obviously ended by the film, actually went on to become a popular magician.

as Jeanne's supposedly redemptive love reflects more her desperation than anything resembling passion. When he asks why she visits, she answers honestly: "You're all I've got." As many have pointed out, the real literary counterpart to Michel might be Camus's Meursault in *The Stranger*, down to his real "crime" being against his mother, and atmospherically, the film calls to mind not so much Dostoyevsky as Beckett or, later, Pinter. Perhaps most importantly, while Michel does confess, he tells Jeanne he only does so in order to retract it later and complicate the case, and there is none of Raskolnikov's final expression of deep remorse.

The musical framing has the same effect, even more indirectly. It faintly suggests, no doubt after several viewings and some research, a psychological dimension again elliptically and atmospherically expressed. Lully (1632–87) was an openly gay member of Louis's court, and his opera *Atys* tells the story of a passionate love that, by violating norms, leads to death, a risk Lully himself ran by being so open. That theme plays over another framing device, the written message that supposedly tells us what the film is about and destroys any suspense about Michel and Jeanne. The musical passage, which recurs several times and ends the film, begins in the opening credits and the scrolling "explanation" for about two and a half minutes.

As has often been pointed out, the intimacy of pickpocketing, especially since the majority of victims in the film are men, and since there is such quiet intimacy among members of the gang, especially between Michel and his chief teacher, Kassagi,[8] all suggest a "real reason," a psychosexual, largely homoerotic reason that Michel becomes obsessed with pickpocketing, and that again suggests that self-opacity is part of the point. The staging of Michel's first meeting with Kassagi makes this point about as clearly as possible within Bresson's stylistic requirements. The meeting is staged very much like a first meeting between potential lovers, and Michel's reaction seems to involve both deep unease and what might be shame at his response. The allusions to the homoerotic are as subtle, even as suppressed as they are in what we "see" of Michel's mindedness: just shots of hands slipping inside men's clothes, the growing regard of Michel and Kassagi's character for each other, available to the viewer only visually, the absence of any discussion of Michel's erotic life, his awkwardness around Jeanne, and of course the clumsiness of their last encounter (figures 3.1 and 3.2).

8. As Indiana (2014) suggests, "Kassagi is like the lover who, after you've had a few quotidian partners, reveals the astonishing range of pleasures available from someone who actually knows what he's doing."

FIGURE 3.1

FIGURE 3.2

Millar is right that the pickpocketing gestures can be viewed as "surreptitious caresses."[9] As we shall see, while the nonprofessional Martin LaSalle does not "perform" the part of Michel, his bearing and especially his eyes slowly create a sense of great self-dissatisfaction. This may of course have a lot to do with his failure to have amounted to much in life, and his shame at having stolen from his mother, but it may have something to do with repressed homoerotic desires, sublimated in the touching and closeness of pickpocketing. Certainly, that scene with Kassagi is staged as an erotic encounter, and we will come to expect a general self-opacity in Michel. This all may have something to do with the oddly chaste and sexless last scene with Jeanne. These are more indications that what matters to him about pickpocketing is not available to him, and so another reason to distrust and avoid explicit psychological expressiveness in the film.

And that is not an isolated point about individual vanity or weakness or self-deceit. In the world that Michel and everyone else lives in, the delusions and self-opacity of all the characters are understandable defenses against a form of life that has become routinized and gone dead. The "atmospheric" effect of Bresson's minimalism is another feature of his style that is not motivated only by minimalist cinematic purity. That atmosphere is suffused with an arid lifelessness, an existential deadness in which anything one can do that can create an erotic (or any other kind of) frisson, life, energy, danger, thrill, is shown to be irresistible. The cinematic capacities for showing the viewer such a world shift our attempt to understand Michel from the expressly psychological to the social or worldly, and this is true of many of his films, especially the film most like *Pickpocket*, *L'Argent*. (We will see later how long Michel can last "going straight" within the resources of the work world, and that world-deadness will help illuminate why crime in such a world is not as horrifically transgressive as in Dostoyevsky but almost admirable. This has something to do with why the details of the pickpocketing craft sometimes look like instruction manuals for the viewers.)[10] The most explicit sexual suggestion occurs with the first pickpocketing at Longchamp, when Bresson does something very rare for him, cutting from the hands to a reaction shot of the face, the clearest way to hint at why "the hand" is doing what it is doing. As Michel's hands slide into the alligator (skin-like) purse and the clasp opens, we see the briefest indication of a thrill or a charge in Michel. It is the only time we see such a reaction, so it stands out, or rather stands in, for all of the thefts. (It is no doubt significant,

9. Millar (1969), 82.

10. This is an unusual aspect of Bresson pursued with great intelligence by Price (2011).

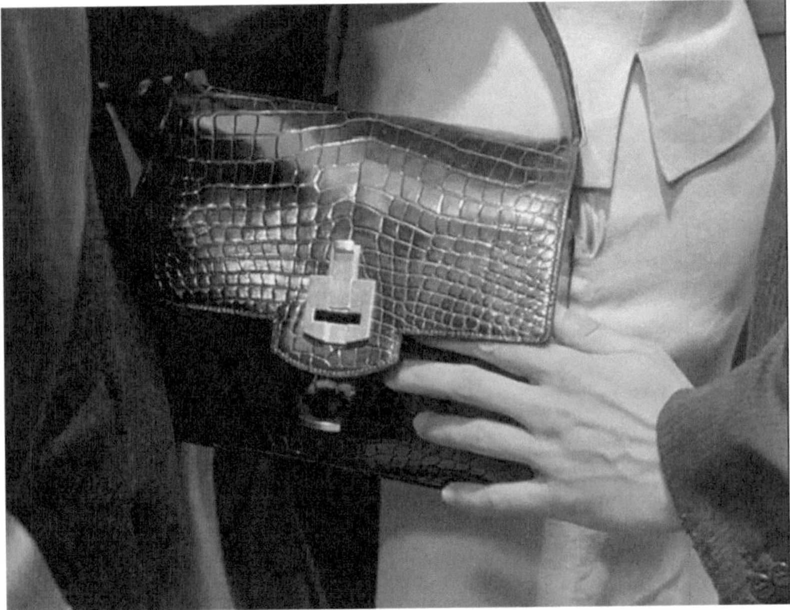

FIGURE 3.3

given his deep and problematic relation to his mother, that while almost all the victims are men, his first attempt is this excited and sexually charged theft from a woman [figure 3.3].)[11]

Finally, there are the two written framing devices, the scroll over at the beginning of the film and the four episodes of Michel writing. We read at the beginning,

> The style of this film is not that of a thriller. Using images and sound the filmmaker (auteur) strives to express the nightmare of a young man whose weaknesses lead him to commit acts of theft for which nothing destined him. However, this adventure and the strange paths it took bring together two souls that may otherwise never have met.

It is certainly true that *Pickpocket* is not a thriller, especially since, like *A Man Escaped*, Bresson gives away the ending immediately; Jeanne and Michel will end up together. But the rest of the preliminary remarks are baffling. We see no evidence of any struggle within Michel to resist the lure of crime, as the claim of "weakness" would imply. He clearly enjoys his

11. If we follow this line, the Inspector then becomes an indispensable father figure, especially since Michel's father is never mentioned in the film.

growing skill and the camaraderie of his gang. (The one instance of weakness falls on the other side of the moral divide. He is at one point too nervous to go through with one of Kassagi's plans to rob a businessman who has just withdrawn cash from a bank.) Further, Michel's comportment throughout is phlegmatic, saturnine, so there is little indication that he is living through a "nightmare" (although at a couple of points he does become quite anxious about being caught). He has rather seamlessly become a criminal, practices his trade assiduously, stops for a while when he is moved by Jeanne's plight (having a baby and being abandoned by Jacques), but this hiatus does not last long. (The practicing, repeating the same thing over and over again so that what is being done becomes invisible, clearly mirrors Bresson's work with actors, attempting to create an automatism in their movements and the line deliveries. The same can be said about Bresson's emphasis on "the hidden," and about his descriptions of what can seem the essential *jouissance* of pickpocketing and his films: "Production of emotion determined by resistance to emotion" [*NC*, 80].) All it takes for him to fall off the straight and narrow is one undercover policeman reading a racing form for him to be moved again to return immediately to Longchamp and his old craft. If anything, this consistency, and his lack of regret—which continues through to the very end of the film—makes one wonder what it could mean to claim that "nothing destined him," as if it was not "in his nature" to live a life of crime. But it seems very much an easy, natural, and perhaps even inevitable role for him to play. As if to confirm this incongruity immediately, after this "explanation" of the film, we see a shot of Michel writing in some sort of remembered account of his life of crime, and there is certainly no indication that he finds himself in some alien world, one where he does not recognize what he has done. There is even a touch of pride in his account. "I know that those who've done these things usually keep quiet, and those who talk haven't done them. Yet I have done them." And we wonder at the claim that except for his criminality, Michel would have never met Jeanne. She is his ill mother's neighbor and de facto caregiver. Michel sees her all the time whenever he visits his mother, and their closeness can be said to begin not because of Michel's pickpocket adventures, but when she learns he stole money from his mother.

The three other writing episodes are also in the past tense. "A week later I sat down in the lobby of a famous bank," but we then see a present-tense enactment of what he had written. "I'd become incredibly audacious. . . . It couldn't last," and we then see the virtuoso pickpocketing episode by the gang in the Gare de Lyon. We do not see his two years in London, but he writes that he returned to Paris penniless, and we see him getting off the train. In fact, this last scene of writing with voice-over casts into some doubt the relation between the recollections and what we see and have seen. Michel writes that he was a successful criminal in London but that he lost all his money at cards and on women. Perhaps, but we have seen nothing before or after the trip to indicate that Michel has any interest at all in womanizing, and while he plays cards with his gang, they do so only to divide up their profits, and while he gambles a bit at the racetrack, he is far more interested in plying his trade there. We begin to become suspicious of the voice-overs too, which recur some sixty times in the film. Browne (1998) sums up the issue well.

> Text is neither a simple commentary on the image, nor is image a simple illustration of the text. Disjunction, independence, interrogation, and even negation of the image, by the sense of the text, is as much a feature as illustration or duplication. (215–16)

He does not mention, but we are allowed to see that in the meantime, Jeanne has had a baby, that Jacques is the father but he has abandoned Jeanne, as has her own father. She is alone and penniless.

Now we might expect that an advocate of "pure cinema" like Bresson would be wary of non-cinematic instructions about how to understand his cinematograph. So why suggest the allusion to Dostoyevsky when that implies a misleadingly elevated significance, a level never reached by the lazy, indifferent pickpocket? And why provide such a misleading set of initial remarks, characterizations that we see almost immediately do not correspond to the images that follow? Perhaps just for that reason; because they invoke a trustworthy reliance on conventional expectations about movies. In this case that would mean an expectation about the intensely theatrical reactions to his crime and the fraught, highly emotional existential self-examination it provokes in Raskolnikov, supposedly Michel's "model," and because we want a plot that follows a clearly delineated genre. We expect to follow instructions: "To be sure, this is not a thriller; it is an adventure that is essentially a 'lovers finding each other' story with a happy ending." Bresson is framing the movie in a way that highlights our relative laziness or our reliance on habit and alerting us to the fact (by what we see rather than what we read) that we should not invoke literary sources or genre conventions; we require a different sort of attentiveness as the cinematograph quickly disabuses us of our expectations about crime movies; thrillers; fated, doomed heroes; and love adventures. The way in which the film affects us is clearly not going to be guided by such framing conventions and will evade the conceptual categorization that habit easily provides. And by suggesting a common frame but with different content, Bresson is also suggesting a contrast between the explicit, expressive psychology of *Crime and Punishment* and the way in which the succession of images can disclose psychological motivation of some complexity even given the robotic delivery and inflectionless line readings. And psychologically, everything at first viewing simply seems mysterious: why Michel begins his pickpocketing; why the Inspector releases him when he is caught with money he cannot account for; why he refuses to see his mother; why he believes himself so superior to others; why he exposes himself to suspicion by telling this theory to the Inspector; what he has been up to during the two years he is away from Paris; and what the final scene with Jeanne, tender but chaste, passionless and ambiguous, could mean. And, as I am trying to suggest throughout, the way in which a cinematic world is available to us invokes a different register of intelligibility—attuned, emotional in a way that breaks through habit to a deeper level of familiarity—and this invites a reappraisal of the possible availability of the human world in ordinary experience. This would be the opposite of the conventional view that Bresson wants to disclose such a world in its possibilities of "transcendence" or in any transcendent supra-human meaningfulness. It is the meaningfulness of *this* world (or its unfulfilled or failed possibility) that Bresson wants to *return* us to, makes us attentive to, not escape.

Michel's points of view about himself, crime, and conventional morality emerge for the most part indirectly, but the heart of the matter, right and wrong, moral or immoral, emerges with Jeanne explicitly. There are two scenes with her that provide what little (and quite indirect) insight we ever get into Michel's state of mind, why the only thing that seems to matter to him is his new craft. The first discussion occurs right after his mother dies and Michel and Jeanne bring her few belongings back to his apartment. Here is their exchange:

> *Michel*: Do you think we will be judged?
> *Jeanne*: Yes, but don't fear for her. She was perfect.
> *Michel*: Judge how? According to laws? What laws? It's absurd.
> *Jeanne*: Do you believe in nothing?
> *Michel*: I believed in God, Jeanne . . . for three minutes.

This all seems a simple expression of nihilism: that is, not just that laws do not apply to superior types, but that the very notion of law is absurd. But the context of the conversation creates a different atmosphere. Michel asks whether we will be judged, and Jeanne assumes he is worrying about the state of his mother's soul. But he has not asked about his mother and seems rather to be still thinking of his guilt over having stolen money from the most important person in his life. His furious insistence that no one should be judged, that the very notion is absurd, seems a defensive reaction, a way of defending himself from his own guilt, and the same complication and unclarity attends to his expression of atheism. Jeanne does not yet know that it was Michel who stole the money, and it starts to become clear in the scene that while Michel may reject the idea of legal and moral principles, it is not true that he cares about nothing. He cares about Jeanne, albeit without yet having admitted that to himself. What begins to matter to him is how he appears in her eyes, as he acts out his shame unknowingly with this display of amoralism. We "see" very little of this in Michel's face or eyes or line delivery, and, as Bresson intends, it is the sequence of images over time that begins to disclose Michel's concerns, concerns he does not appear able to admit to himself.

This becomes even clearer later in the second scene with her when she realizes that he is the one who stole the money from his mother. It takes him a while to get the rather naive and innocent Jeanne to see his guilt, and it must count in some way as a confession, even if hardly yet any repentance.

The police have called Jeanne in for questioning about the reported theft from Michel's mother. But the complaint had been withdrawn, and when Michel learns that it was his mother who withdrew it, he realizes that she knew her son had stolen from her. He asks Jeanne if she knows too, if she can guess and when she hesitates, he says, "Think, you idiot," and the penny drops. "How could you?" she asks (figure 3.4). Despite her horror at what

FIGURE 3.4

FIGURE 3.5

he has done, when she admits that she considers him a thief and he says he will not then shake her hand, she embraces him, that is, accepts what he has done. But it would appear that he still cannot welcome such an acceptance, although again no flicker of self-awareness or detectable guilt surfaces. She asks if he will go, leave town; he says that the idea suddenly seemed possible, says he will not leave and then promptly does.

There is another quite puzzling "scene of writing" in the film, one Bresson highlights at some length three different times, although the commentary on the film by and large ignores it.[12] These are scenes that have at their center Richard Lambert's book on the British pickpocket, con man, actor, and poet George Barrington (1755–1804), *The Prince of Pickpockets* (figure 3.5). The first scene occurs after Michel has joined his gang and become a professional pickpocketer, as it were. He finds his friend Jacques in his room, leafing through the book, and they have a conversation about theft. Jacques is quite critical, accusing Barrington of being an idler and of robbing his friends. He goes on to say that at least Barrington had courage because they used to hang thieves like him. The conversation is charged, and it is likely that the book is a means for Jacques to express his discomfort

12. Quite a valuable exception: Kline (1998).

with what he must suspect is Michel's new livelihood. He knows that Michel does not work, always has money, and he may even have seen him with his new circle of friends.

The book also serves as the same sort of vehicle for unspoken meaning in its final two appearances in scenes with the Inspector. At first, they are in a café, and the Inspector notices the book and asks if Barrington is one of Michel's superior people. He tells Michel to come see him and bring the book. Immediately afterward Michel notes that the Inspector clearly suspects him and he tells Jacques that he realizes that Jacques suspects him too. And here there is a serious connection with Raskolnikov: an apparent, likely unacknowledged desire on Michel's part to be found out, to be stopped. There is after all something comically obvious in a pickpocket carrying around a book about a famous pickpocket in conversations with a friend and with a policeman who both suspect him of being a pickpocket. With this issue there has been a tendency to aestheticize the whole issue of pickpocketing and Barrington (an actor and an artist as well as a thief),[13] and there are such allusions, but the appreciation of Bresson's de-psychologization can go too far. The images we see can show us something about Michel that Michel cannot see, that his claim for superiority is likely a compensation for feelings of worthlessness (especially in the eyes of his mother and Jeanne) and that his bravado and audaciousness express a need to stop that he is not aware of and cannot control. (There is a material embodiment of this throughout the film: the camera points out frequently that Michel never locks his door, sometimes leaves it open, even with all his loot clumsily hidden inside.)[14] The Barrington book is at the same time an expression of his arrogance and of his conscience, and Bresson clearly revels in such contradictions within the soul.

Accordingly, after the café scene, the objects in the scene, the book and the knife, bear the ambiguous meaning of the conversation when Michel visits the detective's office, as requested with the Barrington book. (Michel realizes very quickly that his visit had been a trap, set so that the police can search his room.)

The last time we see the book is when the Inspector comes to Michel's room and lets him know that he knows, even confesses that he has been

13. I think this is true of Kline's (1998) account. He is right though that the complexities of staging and filming the great team-pickpocketing scenes in the Gare de Lyon must have rivaled if not exceeded in complexity the pickpocketing itself. But if Bresson is trying to suggest that pickpocketing is a kind of art form and that his own cinematic art is a kind of pickpocketing, theft, or magic show, what would be the point of such a parallel?

14. Cf. Durgnat (1999), 51.

too lenient with him and wants to explain himself. Michel picks up the Lampert biography and hurls it to the floor, screaming "enough!" as if his inner conflict is now unbearable. The Inspector responds in a fatherly or at least avuncular way. The irony of the scene emerges in its closing lines, which suggest that, although the Inspector wants to open Michel's eyes to himself, his own "intentions" are opaque to him as well. (He still only says that Michel could be arrested not that he now will be.)

We get some sense of the combination of the sexual allure and obsession in Michel's pickpocketing in a scene with Michel, Jacques, and Jeanne on an outing. Jacques and Jeanne want to go on an amusement park ride; Michel stays behind. But all it takes is one glance at an expensive watch on the hand of a neighboring man, and Michel is off. We know he is going to try to steal the watch, but the suddenness of the desire and the impulsive decision to steal it give us some sense of why pickpocketing matters the way it does to Michel,[15] even though he and we cannot spell it out. He gets in trouble this time and has to run away, stumbling, dirtying and tearing his clothes; but at the end of the scene, he proudly displays to himself the precious watch.

Since so much is so indirectly disclosed, and since so little of what we begin to see is available to Michel, or even to the Inspector, the two aspects of Michel's psyche that begin to emerge—the attractiveness to him of pickpocketing or crime in general in the work and social world of postwar Paris and what appears to be the emergence of something like conscience (his concern with Jeanne's view of him and his recklessness, with its implications of a wish to be caught and stopped)—do not permit much material for interpretation. There is no real conventional view of morality as such emerging. Michel never seems to realize that he is taking what belongs to others, ignoring their equal standing in a moral world, no worries about what he might owe to Jeanne, and certainly no concern with God's laws or his own salvation. We only see brief hints of his own unease with himself, but these begin to accumulate sequentially and as they do we become something like "attuned" to who Michel is and why he is acting as he does. Questions about the "real" Michel—Is he really a criminal? Does he really love Jeanne? Is he really guilty about his mother and his crimes? Is he really transformed by Jeanne in the end?—all seem ill formed and misleading. To understand Michel is not to see into his soul or to be able to identify some core self. As with Proust's Marcel, what

15. The suddenness of the desire and the frenzy of the pursuit again suggest a sexual situation.

begins to emerge over time is not the disclosure of anything substantive, but something like the "accent" or inflection with which Michel does and says what he does. (I mean the way in which in Proust's novel Marcel comes to "understand" the composer Vinteuil and how he has changed by "understanding" the different accents and tonality of an earlier sonata when compared to a later.) We cannot formulate propositionally what the exact nature of Michel's unease with himself is, but we cannot deny what the accumulation of his scenes with Jeanne (his concern that she sees him as a thief) and his reckless instigations with the Inspector seem to sound in the same register. This is not traditional guilt (except in the case of his mother, but even in that case, he imagines what she would think of him if she knew, not that he has violated his duty to her) but an accumulated sense, barely registering on him, that he is not who he wants to be, that he is hardly superior, that he is a thief, disloyal to his mother, unable to keep his word to Jeanne and go straight for more than a brief period. The remarkable thing about our awareness of this, or better our growing sensitivity to what makes Michel act as he does, is that none of it ever seems to dawn on Michel in anything like these terms. Even his growing affection for Jeanne is more visible to us than it appears to him. (He blurts out things that reveal himself unknowingly. When he asks Jacques if he loves Jeanne, he tells him that if he loves her, he should buy her gifts, something no doubt in his own mind as a desire for her he unknowingly expresses in that form.) If we need a determinate term for it, the "realization," such as it implicitly is, seems to be that he is living an inauthentic life, the possibility of which is based in his manifest self-deceit, often detectable in his voice-overs and writing. A great achievement of the film is that his sense of this is far less clear to him than it is to us.

When Michel "falls off the wagon," as it were, and returns to where it all began, Longchamp, Michel's discomfort with his new friend, the entrapping policeman from the night before, is palpable. He even notices that the man claims to have won a huge wad of money even though Michel knows that the horse the man bet on did not place in the race. Then, as they watch the next race, he tries by far the most difficult and risky attempt yet: a nearly impossible backward pickpocket. Even after Michel notices that his friend has an evil gleam in his eye, he tries it anyway (figure 3.6).

He is caught, and this time the Inspector does not release him.

The film concludes with two scenes in prison. In the first, Michel is at his most cynical and nihilistic, telling Jeanne that he is only sorry that he got caught, that he cannot stand the idea of letting his guard down, that he cares about nothing and no one. But when she reacts by trying to leave, he immediately tells her to stay. Once again, we see the remarkable capacity

FIGURE 3.6

of human beings both not to mean what they are saying and not to know that they don't mean it. We see, having seen the sequences of images with Jeanne, that he cares a great deal about his standing in her eyes and is defensively protecting himself from shame by his bravado.

There then follows a long period in which she does not visit. (We learn later that her child was ill and that she could not visit.) Michel falls into despair and contemplates suicide, apparently still unaware of the connection with what he says next to himself, "Jeanne did not come back." He receives a letter explaining her absence (he says that his heart pounded as he read the letter), and the last scene is set up.

We hear in the voice-over, "Something lit up her face," and they have a strange caress, more like a sister and brother than romantic partners. He kisses her on the forehead, and she kisses his hands (figure 3.7). This tender scene is deeply ambiguous, besides being somewhat chaste, sexless, and physically peculiar. The bars would not prevent a more romantic kiss on the lips, and her kissing his hands, while it indicates she forgives him for what his hands have been doing, makes the actual geometry of the embrace unusual, to say the least. The dialogue is romantic. He remarks on the strange path he had to take to find her. But the scene is the culmination of the film and should back-shadow its very point, but that point remains unclear. I want to say that such unclarity—that is, the fact that the culminating

FIGURE 3.7

non-embrace embrace evidently means a great deal to both persons even though we cannot say in some determinate form what it means—is continuous with Bresson's suspicions of self-reports and self-understanding in most of his films. This is certainly a breakthrough in Michel's sangfroid, which was not even shaken by his mother's death; but a breakthrough to what?

Commentators on the film though have been quick to fold the ending into a conventional reading of Bresson's cinematographic project as a whole, as expressing a religious sensibility. Here are some examples. First, Tony Pipolo:

> Michel's ability to embrace a healthier life and the love of another presumes recognition and relaxation of the guilt and shame with which he was living, a process, "in which the superego forgives the person who is aware of the misdeeds of sinfulness . . . we call this self-forgiveness. Religion calls it 'grace.'" (Freud, *Beyond the Pleasure Principle*). (Pipolo 2010, 205–6)

Consider the vast extent of the implications drawn here from that unusual embrace. It is of course possible that Bresson could have set up the finale in a way that the viewer comes to understand something deeper and more wide-ranging than the characters yet do, but we know that Michel has already made one commitment to Jeanne that he could not keep, has already said that he has made confessions that he will take back and has known his own mind so little throughout the film that to attribute to him a commitment to a "healthier life" is a fantasy of Pipolo's, not from anything in the film.

The same might be said of Paul Schrader's comment:

> It [the moment with Jeanne] is a "miraculous" event: the expression of love by an unfeeling man within a cold environment, an act which now requires his [the viewer's] participation and approval. Irony can no longer postpone his decision. It is a "miracle" which must be accepted or rejected. (Schrader 2018, 106–7)

But we have seen that the event is not miraculous. Michel's feelings for Jeanne have evolved from gratitude to pity to generosity to a moment when he appears to recognize that her absence in his life (when she ceases to visit) is leading him to suicide. For all we know, he is in the same place she is: she's all he's got. Given the way the meeting with Kassagi was staged, it is impossible not to speculate that the halting, timid physicality of the "embrace," and the fact that there are (and will always remain?) "bars" between them, suggests again a possible doubt on Michel's part about his own sexual identity.

Or this from Joseph Cunneen:

> The "redemption" in Michel is perhaps prepared for by a few fleeting shots in which Bresson suggests that everything is to be understood in relation to the death of his mother, especially since this also brings him close to Jeanne. *Pickpocket* is surely a continuation of the prison theme of *A Man Escaped*, an ongoing meditation on the mystery of grace. (Cunneen 2003, 81–82)

Presumably, Cunneen is persuaded by this view of his sense of the suddenness and perhaps unmotivated character of Michel's change, but Michel is a man alone in prison and when the only person who visits him stops, his realization of the importance of Jeanne need not be brought about by some act of grace, not to mention that virtually anything can be accounted for, if that is the right word, by the mystery of grace.

The same could be said of Jean Collet's comment, when he is discussing those who regard the transformation as too abrupt:

> If this final illumination was caused by some necessity of plot, we would no longer be required to speak of grace. By definition grace is free of any necessity, and hence gratuitous. Isn't that enough to make the conversion of Michel not appear improbable? (Collet 1960, 18)

This obviously assumes (grace) what should be shown, and the remark has an odd inverse logic: anything not compatible with grace must be off track.

And at the most extreme end of such views, Louis Malle's:

> His [Michel's] grandeur is obvious: in the Christian tradition man is the fragment of God, "the deposed king," at once the protagonist and the victim of the great mystery of Grace. That is what gives the film its surprising developments, quick movements, repetitions, contradictions and surprises, its intuitive and learned rhythms, suggesting the irregular beatings of a heart.
>
> "The ways of God are impenetrable" [Pascal]. (Malle in Arnaud 1986, 37)

Such views seem to me reductive and forced. Much closer to the mark is T. Jefferson Kline:

> Perhaps this is why the final images of the film focus on Michel carefully separated from Jeanne by iron bars. . . . What a strange path, through Dostoevsky and George Barrington Bresson has taken in order (not) to tell us his story. (Kline 1998, 266)

But this is still put too strongly. The point has not been to avoid telling us the story of Michel, but to avoid telling it under assumptions about self-knowledge and knowledge of others that Bresson clearly thinks are naive. The point is not that Michel lacks self-consciousness or is literally an automaton, as if Bresson were a behaviorist, but that self-knowledge—or in this case what Michel understands is happening when he embraces Jeanne—is not self-inspection or self-"insight." It is a matter of self-interpretation and even at that is not a person's search for a discursive formulation that can be asserted in judgments. It is more a matter of someone's being attuned to themselves, in which what one does is experienced as one's own or strange, alienated and in that sense not understood. So to attribute all these extensive implications to Michel from this moment with Jeanne—repentance, reform, an outpouring of heterosexual and thus reassuring love, the religious experience of grace—as if Michel will now serve out his prison term and get a working-class job to support Jeanne and her baby, is wildly speculative and at great odds with the way that the film has treated Michel's mindedness and what we have seen of the world in which any such mindedness would be possible.

And it is not as if Michel in particular is simply unusually bad at self-awareness. Bresson's ambition is not to tell a story about a peculiar, diffident pickpocket but, in his terms, the truth about what it is and what it is not to know one's own mind in some historical environment. In this regard,

Michel is treated as typical. What it means to him to experience what he does in that last scene is simply not formulable in any new project or resolve, any more than what it meant to him to be a criminal is something withheld from us by Bresson's de-psychologized style. There simply are not punctuated moments of self-knowledge with such extensive entailments. As we have been seeing, such experiences are not propositionally structured, as Bresson pursues his project of exploring how human beings can come to be "onto" meaningfulness, sense in their lives, or fail to find it, fail in determinate ways to find it. At best there are new possibilities that depend on what happens next, what Jeanne ultimately does, how long Michel must be in prison, what kind of job Michel gets, or even what the work world in Paris becomes in the early sixties. In general, the model of some determinate inner resolve, then executed to have an effect on the world, is consistently treated by contrast as phenomenologically simplistic since the world and one's being-in-the-world have already set the horizon of the possible meaning of any such resolve. And this is a state of affairs that surely can only be shown not said, disclosed in a way that invites critical attentiveness but not with any possible goal like those behind the quotations we have just seen. And what is shown is left in a state far more uncertain than the commentators allow. In the first place, it would be hard to point to this scene as evidence that Michel's self-centeredness, his laughable claims to be a superior type and his narcissism have been overcome by Jeanne's fidelity. Given what we have seen, there is every reason to believe that Michel will remain Michel, happy that he has attached himself to someone whose relation to him may be more motherly than romantic. For another, there is an odd tonality to the ending that I cannot reproduce here. As their faces are pressed to the bars, we hear the Lully theme again, but this time a lighthearted, bouncy segment that lends almost an air of the comic to the ending—not so much "they will live happily ever after," but "and so our two heroes unite, clueless about what they are doing and what will come."

4
Balthazar's World

Au hasard, Balthazar is in narrative terms a dual plot film, and as in all dual plot narratives, the two are parallel and linked, each meant to shed light on the meaning of the other. One narrative depicts the fate and suffering of a donkey, Balthazar. Among other associations, Balthazar is traditionally taken to be the name of one of the three magi who visited the newborn Jesus. That status, as a witness, perhaps even as a figure for the director himself, is an important point by ironic contrast. What Balthazar witnesses in this world is unremitting depravity and evil, not the birth of a god. Besides that, another possible source is the story of Lucius in Apuleius's *The Golden Ass*, and another is the one Bresson cites, the account by Myshkin in Dostoevsky's *The Idiot*, when he relates how a donkey's braying relieved his depression. The other story depicts the fate and sufferings of a village girl, Marie, whom we see as a young girl and as an adolescent. One signal of the link between the two narratives occurs several times in the film when Marie's father is looking for her and repeatedly calls out her name in a braying way—"MarIE, MarIE"—which echoes the braying we hear from Balthazar several times. In fact, Bresson takes a big risk when, in the opening credits, during Schubert's piano sonata, he interrupts the beautiful sound with Balthazar's braying, thus risking a comic effect both to suggest the connection between the sonata's atmospheric mood and Balthazar's fate, but also to place Balthazar's voice on some sort of aesthetic plane with the piano piece. Balthazar is by turns a pet; a beast of burden and farm animal; again a pet and of service to Marie's family; a baker's donkey used for deliveries; owned by a drunkard, Arnold, to give rides on tourist tours; a circus animal; Arnold's again; cruelly mistreated by a grain merchant; again Marie's domestic animal; and finally stolen by the most evil character in the film,

Gérard, and used to smuggle merchandise across the border with Spain, where Balthazar is shot and killed.

Marie's fate is likewise miserable. Her childhood friendship and later romance with the son of the first owners of Balthazar, Jacques, is ruined by her father's bitter and catastrophic dispute with Jacques's family. She enters, often confused and conflicted, into a relationship with the hoodlum and sadist Gérard. Even more confused and conflicted, and desperate to obtain the money she would need to escape the village, she offers herself one night to a miserly grain merchant for enough money to get away. An attempted renewal of her bond with Jacques first fails, then appears to succeed as she resolves to face down and break with Gérard and his gang. This does not end well. The gang strips and abuses, probably rapes Marie, and she disappears from the film, likely dies by her own hand. (Throughout the story of Marie, the mindedness of characters is apparently as opaque to them as it is to us; it is nearly impossible to discover intentions, motivations, or any self-reflective moments at all. Marie's inconstancy and inconsistency are major features of the film.)

Interwoven throughout the main two narratives are several subplots, and these and the two main plots intersect each other so frequently and unexpectedly that it is almost impossible to follow a continuous narrative line.[1] Much of the editing appears *au hasard*, as much as chance events—like the apparent death or immanent death of the daughter in Jacques's family at the beginning; the sudden appearance of a new owner, the village drunk, Arnold, when Balthazar almost dies; Arnold's miraculous inheritance—all drastically impact the lives involved. The original owners of Balthazar and of the vacation home and farm that Marie's father eventually farms for them begin the film in an eerie vignette, an illness and probably the death of the youngest child. This sad event is the reason the vacationing family never returns. (This scene is a fine illustration of how the minimalization of expressivity can heighten rather than reduce the emotional impact of the images. The absence of any visible reaction to the child's fate, perhaps death, concentrates all the emotional power of the scene in the briefest indication of the terrible lifelessness of the child [figure 4.1], and then the sudden shock when we as well as the characters are suddenly propelled out of this childhood world by the crack of a whip, a violent shift to a world of thoughtlessness, cruelty, avarice, gluttony, pride, greed, lust, not to mention hopelessness and despair [figure 4.2]. The scene is also typical of

1. "Whereas up to now [in *Pickpocket*, for example], everything happened as if you were following a single thread. Here [*Balthazar*] there are several threads at once." Bresson (2013), 141.

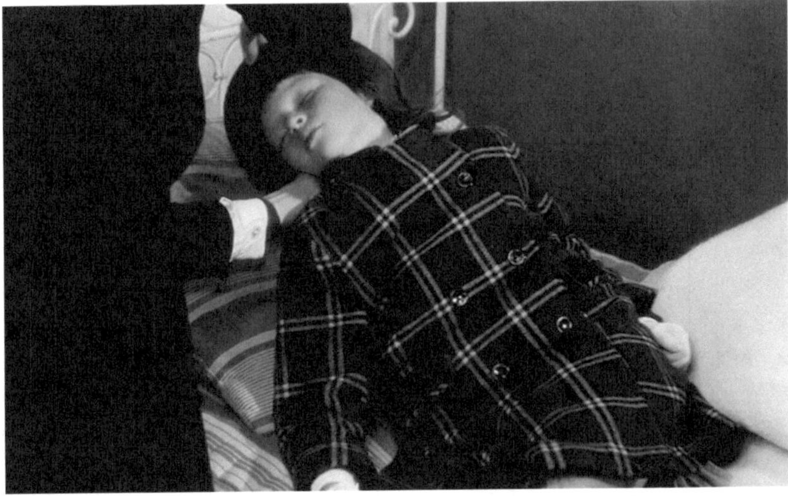

FIGURE 4.1

FIGURE 4.2

Bresson's frequent use of ellipses. We leap ahead more than a dozen years to when Marie is sixteen, and the events that follow seem to last about a year.)

This later period is when Marie's involvement with a local hoodlum, the black-jacket-clad Gérard, and his gang begins. That beginning is ominous. We are introduced to the gang in an act of mindless mischief. They are slicking down a road with oil so that cars speeding past will spin out, all apparently just for their own amusement although their expressions remain deadpan. While they are waiting for another car, they come upon Marie and her father in their donkey cart and ride alongside, mocking them for still using a cart, commenting ironically on how "modern" the use of donkeys is. (Balthazar's world is much closer to the older village world, where a dependent life between humans and domesticated animals, the intersection of worlds, was experienced.)[2] Gérard keeps eyeing Marie uncomfortably until her father speeds them along, and the gang stops to watch a car skid and spin out. They watch impassively, do not laugh or respond. Another car drives by and this time Bresson does not even cut to the crash; we hear only the sound. Remarkably, none of the gang bothers to watch the results of their vandalism. Their actions seem totally pointless, simple meaningless malevolence. This introduction of Gérard is apt since it foreshadows other scenes of his sadism. When he is working for the bakery, delivering bread with Balthazar, frustrated that the stubborn donkey won't at one point move on, he wraps newspaper around his tail and lights it on fire. I am not sure how the scene was filmed, but the staging is painfully realistic; it looks very much like Balthazar's tail is on fire and that he suffers accordingly. As with all his other suffering, there is no way for him to resist what happens to him, subject as he is to the whims of the human world. In the parallel plot structure this points us to Marie's fate as well. She is as trapped in the village as Balthazar; all her possibilities are delimited by the village world, and she comes to a point where she will do anything to escape, as we shall see.

Another subplot involves Marie's father's ruinous relation with Jacques's family. He changes careers from a schoolteacher to farmer and actually becomes quite successful (and extremely proud of himself, that he learned it all "from books"),[3] so successful that rumors start that he is cheating the owner, who then demands that the father produce the records of the farm's business. The father claims he is insulted by this lack of trust, refuses to compromise, and ends up ruining his family's life. (The film strongly hints that the father *has* actually cheated the owner. He tells his wife that he cannot produce his receipts because he has not kept them, but we are shown that he has all of them.)

2. See Browne (1977) on this point, 28. In general, though, Browne wants the film to be a religious allegory. "The film in its most general significance undertakes to testify to a religious truth: there is a divinity behind the chance events of life and suffering of man. The problem of the construction of the film is to authenticate this claim" (21). This is a typical interpretation, indeed canonical, but I see no evidence for this in what Browne appeals to in the article.

3. The symbol of his new, modern farming methods—which makes him much more efficient than his neighbors and prompts the envy that will ruin his life—is his tractor, and later his automobile.

There is a strange and one-sided attraction between a middle-aged baker's wife and the nefarious Gérard. There is a mysterious murder investigation that we learn little about, but both Arnold and Gérard's gang appear to be suspected. Bizarre conversations about painting and agent responsibility occur during one of Arnold's guided tours of the Pyrenees. Balthazar briefly escapes and is captured by a circus, where he becomes part of a phony "animal genius act," and is recaptured by Arnold. Arnold suddenly inherits a fortune, promptly gets drunk, falls off Balthazar and dies. Throughout the two main narratives and these subplots, the film shows us a village in a modernizing transition, from donkey carts to automobiles, from plows to tractors, the intrusion of modern regulatory bureaucracy into rural farm life, a youth culture now fixated on transistor radios, motorbikes, parties fueled by alcohol and sex, and a general environment aptly summarized in perhaps the basic bourgeois maxim by the miserly grain merchant: "I love money, and I hate death." This is a theme occasionally in the film itself, as in Gérard's comments on donkeys and his own love of motorbikes and gadgets. Throughout the film, and especially at the end, the only non-diegetic music we hear is the andante movement from Schubert's penultimate piano sonata (D959), a moving berceuse or lullaby-like section that seems associated with regret at both Balthazar's and Marie's loss of innocence and their first exposure to the world aptly summed up by that merchant.

Another framing device for the film is its beginning and its end, and this introduces the notion of a world. At the beginning the baby donkey Balthazar is in his world, the animal world, being nursed by his mother, surrounded by sheep whom we barely see, their presence signaled by their tinkling bells. The film begins with him being torn from that world for the amusement of the children who find him cute and want him as a pet. (The intrusion of one world into another is signaled by a human arm intruding into the animal world.) The film ends with Balthazar, after all of his suffering in the human world, returning to the comfort of that original animal world, dying amid and clearly comforted by a large flock of sheep. Around the middle of the film, he returns to an animal world in a different way when, after escaping from a beating by Arnold, he is taken in by a circus and there is a justly famous depiction of some sort of mutual intelligibility among the animals, as if acknowledging to each other that this intersection of worlds is not where they belong, in cages and performing tricks. It is almost as if the circus animals are warning Balthazar to get out while he can (figures 4.3 and 4.4).

This contrast between worlds is what allows features of those worlds that would not otherwise be available to become indirectly accessible. The notion of world in such a claim is, on the one hand, very familiar—if we

FIGURE 4.3

FIGURE 4.4

refer to the world of indigenous natives, or the world of rural villages, the world of Balthazar, we know we do not mean the totality of encounterable objects, but, as discussed in chapter 1, something like a horizon of possible meaningfulness, a historical context that delimits what could matter to human beings at a time, and what could not, what enterprises simply would not make sense. This idea of an always already deeply presupposed horizon of possible contextual significance is not something that could ever be an object in a world because such a world is a condition for anything showing up meaningfully in experience at all. Everything we encounter in a historical world makes a kind of immediate, familiar sense, pre-reflectively. Immediate and pre-reflective because this familiarity is not a matter of applying norms, rules, or conventions. But the world of such possible meaningfulness is itself not so encounterable. This original mode of meaningfulness is not originally a matter of conceptual classification or perceptual discrimination, but a far more direct form of everyday, taken-for-granted familiarity. We do not first encounter perceptually discriminated objects and then bestow significance. The idea of such a two-step procedure is not phenomenologically credible (any more than a string of sounds is first heard as such and then interpreted as language). Entities and others in our experience show up, are salient, because of their degrees of significance in the practical tasks a human being engages in, courses of action that are possible, could make sense, at a time.

For an example, consider an animal world. An animal species is, like us, not just visually attentive to everything perceptually present. What emerges as salient (prey, predator, shelter, mate) and what does not, what means nothing to them (highways, power lines, planets), so emerges because of its species form.[4] The suggestion is that how elements of our experience emerge as salient is as well a function of their mattering within a historical world's horizon of possible (and impossible) mattering, but without at all being limited to our biological species form. This all means, as incomplete as such an account is, that when we ask about the human world the characters inhabit in *Au hasard, Balthazar*, we ask not about what beliefs they have about what matters—given Bresson's obvious doubts about self-deceit and self-opacity, that would be pointless—but what the camera can show emerges as the context of significance that seems to inform and guide the decisions and actions and experiences of the characters, even, paradoxically, if that context is failed meaningfulness, a depiction of absence. (This is a failure that forms a frame for the film: Gérard's pointless destructiveness at the beginning in the scene with cars, and at the end when he destroys a bar during a party.) How being in such a world bears on possible courses of action is a major issue in all his films. That is, I want to say, what Bresson is trying to show us cinematographically.

As noted several times already, it is in this sense that some frequently ask if the horizon of worldly significance in Bresson should be understood

4. Gianopolou (2024) has an illuminating discussion of the circus scene. She wants to attribute ethical agency to Balthazar and so emphasizes the "ocular intensity" (12) of the scene. I agree and think we understand even more of the animal's vitality and ethical relevance by understanding animal "worlds" and their contrast and similarities with the human.

to be religious, either by its presence in *Angels of Sin, Diary of a Country Priest*, and *The Trial of Joan of Arc*, or putatively by *that* absence, in films like *Mouchette, Une femme douce, The Devil, Probably*, which feature suicides, or *L'Argent*, which ends in senseless mass murder. Balthazar, for instance, is sometimes understood to be a kind of Christ figure, silently taking on and witnessing the burden of human depravity, until stoically bearing that burden leads to his (perhaps) sacrificial death. Pipolo (2010), for example, confidently asserts that "Balthazar reaffirms the uniqueness and otherness of Christ, his mysterious, unattainable perfection" (187). And Quandt (2009a) lists, skeptically, the allusions that are supposed to reinforce that association: Balthazar has seven masters, an allusion perhaps to the seven deadly sins, the seven words on the cross, the seven sacraments; the mock baptism the children perform; the smuggler's gold and perfume as the offerings of the magi; the wine that Arnold drinks and the bread that Gérard delivers.[5]

And it can certainly look like several Jansenist commitments are evident in the films, if that is what one is looking for: the utter and unreformable sinfulness of human beings, predestination, salvation as a gratuitous, arbitrary gift of grace, never earned. But while there is certainly unremitting depravity in many of Bresson's films, especially this one, where he appears to want to take us on a tour of types of human depravity, as if a tour of all the deadly sins, he is more sensitive to the attractions of selfishness, indifference, and resentment in the particular historical worlds he is trying to depict, as his concentration on changing features of that world attest. And there is certainly no universal sinfulness and depravity in Bresson's films. Marie is well-meaning if also confused; her mother is saintly; Jacques is weak and naive, not sinful; and Arnold is more of a comic than a base character. The fatalism need not be a religious doctrine either, but the consequence of there being very little in the way of concrete alternate possibilities in such a world, and "grace," which is only stated as such in *Diary*, could just as easily be an indication of the unexpected emergence of ways of mattering that could "by chance" (*au hasard*) drastically change or even redeem a boring or wasted life, or, in failing, provoke despair like Marie's.

For another, in *Balthazar*, the direct allusions to religion seem heavily qualified, quoted as it were, rather than appealed to. Right after the children take possession of Balthazar, for example, they stage their own religious ceremony, solemnly baptizing Balthazar, lighting candles, praying that he "receive the salt of wisdom" and feeding him the sacred salt. The ceremony

5. As noted, Quandt is skeptical of these supposed illusions and rightly notes that "the transcendental reading of the film ignores the pessimism of Bresson's vision," 83.

hardly seems genuinely religious though and is likely ironic—a faint suggestion that baptism itself is childish and useless, not to mention the fact that animals are not born in original sin and do not need to be baptized. The early emphasis on the innocence and happiness of the children—as innocent as Balthazar—does not call out for the washing away of any sin. The only "fall" we see is the fall into the profane adult world.

The one scene inside a church serves only to emphasize the superficiality and untrustworthiness of religious practices, since the sadist Gérard is capable of singing like an angel; he is a choirboy, likely the chief choirboy. When Marie's father is dying the priest who comes to comfort him offers a few platitudes that do nothing to comfort the father or be of any use at all to his wife. In fact, the exchange between them is quite strange. The father, who had seemed hale and healthy, appears to be suddenly dying from his crushed pride and his humiliation at what has happened to his daughter. The priest, at a loss for what to say, opens the Bible and begins reading a passage that says that the father must forgive everyone, as he who has suffered so will be forgiven. The father remarks coldly that he has not suffered that much, a strangely dismissive remark, hardly pious at the end of his life and clearly meant to reject the comfort offered.

In fact, the scene of the dying father and the priest, just about two and half minutes long, is a kind of case study in what Bresson is trying to achieve. The father has been devastated by what has happened to Marie and is ready to "turn his face to the wall" and die. (The treatment of his hands in the scene is also quite powerful [figure 4.5].) He is dying of despair, and his wife summons the priest, telling him, "He is in despair. Comfort him." There are no tears, no wailing, no wringing of hands, no music. The whole scene is deadly quiet and still. The priest clearly does not know what to say and picks up a Bible and reads two passages. As just noted, the father does not respond to the forgiveness passage as if comforted. When the priest reads the second passage, an even more intense pathos is created, again "quietly." "The Lord does not forsake forever. He may punish, yet he will have compassion. He does not willfully afflict the children of men." His wife hears this, believes it, goes outside and prays accordingly. They have lost all their money, their daughter has likely committed suicide, and now her husband is dying. She prays, "Don't take him from me, too.[6] Wait. You know how sad and miserable my life will be." In effect she is counting on the

6. We only have two indications of Marie's fate. After the assault, when Jacques comes to see her, the mother descends the stairs from her room and says that Marie will never come back, and we have this indication of her disappearance as death, "Don't take him from me, *too*."

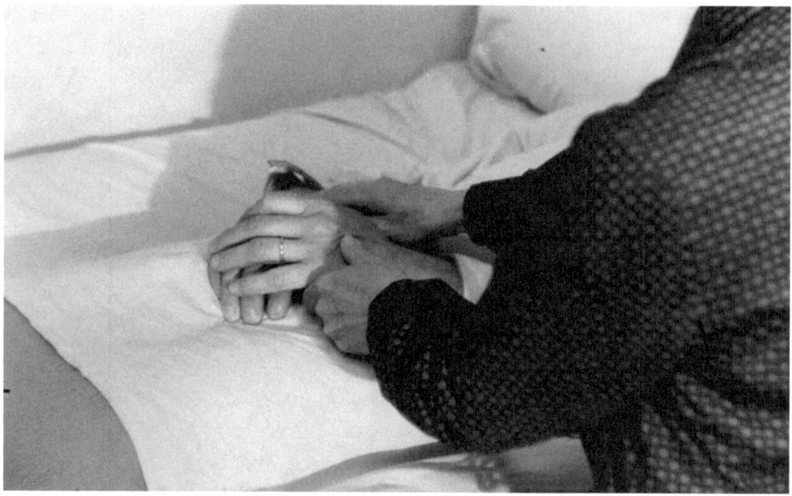

FIGURE 4.5

priest's words, and at that very moment, in a rather cold announcement of her husband's death, the priest knocks on the window with the sad news. (It would seem a simple kindness to come outside and get her.) The very unusual stillness of the scene manages also to create a final overall impression for the viewer—the silence of God.

And when Balthazar appears outfitted in religious decorations, likely for the funeral of Marie's father, the impression is clownish, not devout. This all could still be said to be consistent with the paradoxical presence of the absence of religiosity, that it seems not have any real grip in the town, but one would still need to discuss how *that* failure in particular might bear on the possibilities or lack of them in the world we see. Finally, while it is possible to see Balthazar as Christlike in being "too good for this world" and so doomed to die a "saint" as Marie's mother says, he ends up dying burdened not with the sins of the world but with contraband consumer goods; he resists his role whenever he can, and he dies in a senseless way that makes clear there will be no resurrection.

I have suggested that Bresson's accomplishment is to have discovered a cinematic form that can disclose the meaning or the failure of meaning in persons' lives by shifting our attention away from self-avowed psychological attitudes, away from what characters think about themselves and others, if they ever do (and this is rare in this film), and to draw attention to the common historical world these characters inhabit, the sedimentation of possible meaning they are attuned to in a pre-reflective way and that the camera and sound, used as Bresson does, can capture elements of this dependent mindedness in a distinctive way. This is to be understood as deriving from a horizon of possible significance, a source of mattering that is not a matter of beliefs or commitments but a nondiscursive orientation from possibilities that might make sense or not in a world, and that might become quite meager. This means that the cinematic depiction of this collective attunement is, at least as Bresson sees it, also largely nondiscursive, what Bresson calls "emotional," without the "intervention of intelligence." This does not mean that the characters do not evince attitudes, beliefs, desires, and so forth, but they rarely seem to be reflective subjects of such attitudes, but rather in a way subject to them. Of course, one cannot have a belief or desire without knowing that one does, but such an awareness is normally understood to open up the possibility of asking oneself such things as whether one actually believes what one takes oneself to believe, whether one should, or why one wants something, or what actually matters to one. But why Gérard acts as he does, why Marie's father will not compromise, what the baker's wife wants from Gérard, why Arnold saves Balthazar, why Marie changes her mind about Jacques, do not seem to be questions that are available to the characters, although they are certainly available for us. The actions are not unmotivated, but the air of mystery surrounding their actions demands something new from us, something more interrogative than passive. Again, the cinematic technique expresses a philosophical commitment: a depiction of ordinary life in which a kind of self-forgetfulness, self-opacity, hierarchies of mattering that are not driven by reflective attitudes about what ought to matter, or even what actually matters to one, but which rather seem to be inheritances of a common world that ever more narrowly limits what could matter. (It would not be extravagant to say that as Bresson's work develops, the subject of his last film, *L'Argent*, is the nadir of this historical narrowing and something like its catastrophic culmination: meaning as money.)

Instead of appealing to expressivity, whether in language or even in intonation, facial expressions, and so forth, Bresson portrays what would normally be considered the attitudes and desires of characters in an "external" way, as if those supposed "inner" states are actual only externally, in the public world we see. Available but not transparent; they are possible sources of interpretation. Most often this is available only in what the characters simply do, although any access, for them and for the viewer, to why they do what they do, to their intentions, seems unavailable. One major disclosure of the characters' mindedness, the things they find mattering to them, is Balthazar himself, who functions not just as a witness, but as a kind of screen on which what is at issue for characters is projected. In some cases, "scapegoat" cases we can say, Balthazar is treated as if he were the cause of some character's mistake, failure, or misdeed, a vehicle for what would have been psychological or verbal expression. The most obvious is a rare instance of humor in the film, when a farmer driving a load of hay pulled by Balthazar drives the cart carelessly and too fast, recklessly overturns, and then not only seeks out Balthazar to punish him as if he were at fault, but collects a group of his comrades to hunt down Balthazar, all as if a village mob out for Frankenstein. Arnold tries to beat Balthazar with a chair in what appears to be his own rage at himself for vowing not to drink and then failing in his resolve. Balthazar is sold by Marie's father out of the same false pride that leads him to destroy his family's lives (he thinks owning a donkey makes him look ridiculous), without any sense that he knows what he is doing and why. The simple, pathetic sight of Balthazar waiting as always, patiently, in the snow while Marie and Gérard carry on their assignations, a sign of their indifference to him, their not caring, is a measure of the obsessiveness and self-destructive character of their involvement visible to us but not to Marie. The grain merchant's indifference to any moral restraint, one could say the state of his soul, is "visible" in the sight of Balthazar worked nearly to death by him, starved and beaten, and what appears to be an unmotivated reversal in his narcissism, manifested in his returning Balthazar to Marie's family. Gérard's frustration at his first failed seduction of Marie is projected onto Balthazar as he beats him gratuitously (as Marie, opaque and confused as ever, looks on.)

That first attempted seduction occurs at night in a garden, and is a different sort of projection, as Balthazar also serves as a transitional object for Marie's emerging sexuality. (The convergence of sexual desire and love is rare in Bresson's films.) What is striking in the scene is that neither of them, Marie nor Gérard, hidden from but aware of each other, seems consciously minded in any determinate way (much like Balthazar, obviously). It is very unlikely that Marie has any knowledge of what she is doing as she decorates and caresses Balthazar, and the two, Marie and Gérard, move toward each other deliberately but not quite intentionally and they separate the same way. Marie adorns Balthazar with flowers as if a beloved, projecting herself into a fantasy of romance at once childish and provocative (it goes so far as a kiss), and she is clearly aware of the presence of someone else in the garden, and we suspect, given her remaining there, that she knows it is Gérard. She then sits demurely on a bench as if waiting his approach. Again, we see only a hand as he reaches toward her (figure 4.6). (This prefigures a moment in his successful "conquest" of Marie where the hand functions much less tentatively and in an ugly way [figure 4.7].) As soon as she senses the hand, she pulls away and rushes inside,

FIGURE 4.6

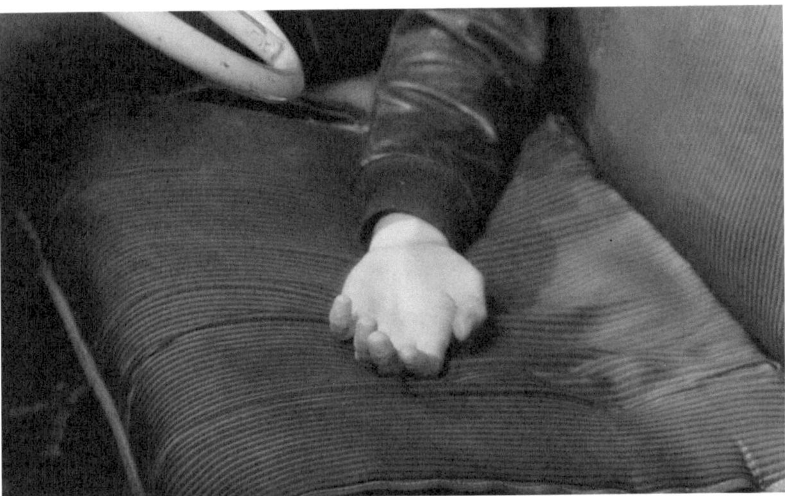

FIGURE 4.7

but keeps the door cracked and watches Gérard wildly beat Balthazar as if he were responsible for the failed seduction. It is as if Gérard is angry and frustrated in what seems a purely reactive rather than determinately motivated way. Balthazar is not conceivably his rival and has had nothing to do with Marie's actions, despite his vulgar fantasies at the beginning of the scene. All we can assume is that he seems to want to punish Marie by beating her pet, although his anger does seem to have something to do with jealousy.[7]

In the conventional philosophical distinction between what I do and what happens to me, where the former is marked out by reflective intentions, and the latter by such notions as drives, instincts, evolutionary imperatives, and being causally acted on rather than acting, the scene, with so little visual evidence of intention or planning, would probably be characterized by some version of the latter sort of explanation. But the duality in question does not make room for what we see, someone who does not have any clear sense of why they are doing what they are doing but who is not impelled or driven. Marie is acting deliberately but not knowingly, another indication of Bresson's distrust of the results of reflective consciousness in human affairs.

Bresson's ability to present characters whose actions are mysterious but not unintelligible is on view in the two strangest subplots in the film, and in neither case is it immediately clear what bearing the scenes have on the central intersection of the animal and human historical worlds or the untrustworthiness of self-understanding and its implications for our understanding of the characters and their understanding of each other. In one, Gérard begins work for a baker and his wife, who have bought Balthazar as a pack animal. Gérard will use him to deliver the bakery's baguettes around the village. But the baker's wife, who is easily old enough to be Gérard's mother, clearly forms a strong erotic attachment to Gérard and begins to treat him as a lover, buying him expensive gifts (a transistor radio and a new motorbike), overlooking his petty theft, promising him money, and she becomes very jealous of his relation to Marie, insisting that the presents will stop if he keeps seeing her. Gérard of course ignores this warning and does not try to hide his meetings with Marie and in general treats the older woman with bemused contempt.

Typically, we are given no access to the wife's point of view. We never learn how she understands her romantic infatuation for Gérard, what it means to her, why it matters to her. Although this is in keeping with Bresson's style in general, in this case it is also clearly because she doesn't understand any of that either, has no real point of view except that she desperately

7. See Gianopolou's (2024) commentary on the garden scene. Especially, "If this is a love scene, Marie is betraying Balthazar even as she is loving him; she looks away from him when she hears a sound nearby, and her hand moves from her heart to the bench to meet another hand. . . . Balthazar . . . is a screen for the projection of an idea or ideal that awakens in her a desire for something absent," 11.

wants to help and to be regarded by Gérard. But we do know that her attraction blinds her completely to Gérard's twisted character. When he is summoned to the police for questioning, she assumes the worst, that he will be arrested, and immediately promises to become his accomplice in crime, to hide him and smuggle him out of the country. She weeps with anxiety for him and begs him not to mock her, which, with his expression, he of course does.

So, there are two female characters involved with Gérard: the baker's wife and Marie. And the contrast seems important. Both are under no illusions about who Gérard is and what he is capable of, but that issue is a live one with Marie, in contrast with the baker's wife's desperately "all in" attitude, making mysterious the question of why Gérard should emerge from the wife's experiences as so important to her, even as she clearly realizes (or, let us say, "feels") his manipulativeness, predation, intimidation, and violence. We sense that she is both pulled toward him and repelled by him. In Marie's case the meaning of her attraction is wrapped up with her growing desperation to find a way to leave the village, her sense that there is no place for her there. In this, there is another link with Balthazar; the village world is not his, nor is it hers. She cannot recognize herself in it, and Gérard, for both women, seems to be a way to refuse to carry on as if there were. He is their transgressive moment. The wife's attraction is no doubt wrapped up in some fantasy about the future, and perhaps because she imagines herself within that fantasy, she is not afraid of Gérard's violence and faithlessness. (She is also unconcerned with Gérard's criminality and guilt, and indeed no general moral considerations seem to get a grip anywhere in the village we see, least of all with respect to Balthazar or his avatars in the film.) But Marie seems both pulled toward Gérard and deeply repulsed by and afraid of him at the same time. As we shall see, she clearly senses that any closeness to him is dangerous and, at some conscious level, wants nothing to do with him.

And typically in Bresson, he is able to show us the manifestations of her complicated, even contradictory mindedness, without guiding us toward any clear sense of her own view of what is happening, although we can see that she has no such clear view. The crucial scene occurs alongside a road where Gérard has tied up Balthazar and is waiting for Marie, knowing she will stop for him. Marie now has her father's car and does stop.

When Marie crosses the road to Balthazar, Gérard slips into the passenger seat of the car. Marie demands that he get out, but he ignores her and sits there threateningly. So, she starts to stalk off. And then the confusing mix of motives becomes apparent, and she stops, turns around, and returns to the car. Gérard has placed his open hand on the seat where she would have to sit, as if inviting her to sit on his hand. He removes it and she gets in, wary but willing in some sense. (She has not run away; he has not threatened her.) She starts the car to drive off, but he turns it off. (That *is* threatening.) He puts his hand on her lap and begins to move it up her body toward her breasts, as she silently submits, weeping quietly. When he puts his hand on her neck, she bolts from the car and runs to Balthazar and hides behind him. Once again, Balthazar serves as a transitional object from adolescent to adult sexuality, as well as a screen on which this tension is projected. They begin to play a bizarre childhood game, as if tag, circling Balthazar, chasing each other as if in fun. The tone between them seems lighthearted, but we hear the Schubert sonata again, in this context giving the scene a melancholic even fatalistic tone, suggesting a deeper meaning than just lighthearted fun. As Marie runs away, she either stumbles or lies down. In any case she does not get up and continue to run. They stare at each other calmly, then walk back to the car. There is an ellipsis; we don't see what happens in the car, but it is announced when their liaison is over as Gérard, with typical vulgarity, announces his "victory" by blasting his baker's horn (figures 4.8, 4.9, and 4.10). This begins their sexual relationship, most of which takes place at an abandoned cabin on her father's farm throughout the winter in rest of the film.

The complexity of her relation to Gérard is evident in another scene where Gérard and his gang are beating up Arnold. Marie tries to stop them and actually slaps Gérard. He of course slaps her back, but yet they reconcile quickly, walking off arm in arm, as if nothing had happened.

FIGURE 4.8

FIGURE 4.9

FIGURE 4.10

Arnold, the town drunk, figures in several subplots of his own. He first emerges after Marie and Gérard's neglect of Balthazar has left the donkey ill and dying. Arnold shows up and claims he can cure him, and he does, using him and another donkey to give tourists rides through the mountains near the village.[8] Second, he plays a major role in the investigation that

8. He tells a villager that being on the road cured Balthazar.

prompted the summons to Gérard. A murder has been committed and the chief suspects appear to be Arnold, although he does not seem capable of murder, and Gérard's gang, who certainly do seem capable; we have seen Gérard's gun. (We learn nothing about the details of the murder, the victim, etc.) Arnold is worried, however. He blacks out when he drinks, and he cannot be sure of what he does during those blackouts. This comes to a head when the gang plants a gun in Arnold's room as the police arrive, clearly hoping there will be an exchange of gunfire, Arnold will be killed, and the police will be tempted to call the murder solved. This does not happen. And finally, at the end of the movie Arnold inherits a fortune from a distant relative, throws a town party, gets very drunk, rides off on Balthazar, falls, hits his head, and dies.

This can all seem like so much extraneous noise in the film, far away from, and a distraction from, the central Marie-Balthazar plots. But Bresson makes use of each of these Arnold moments to intimate something that bears on that theme. The first, the tours Arnold gives with Balthazar, offer occasions for bizarre conversations among the customers, almost a very rare moment of comedy in Bresson. There are two conversations between two pairs of customers: the first about painting, the second about criminal liability. In the first, the two riders pass by a waterfall, and the painter says, "Then onto my canvas burst a multitude of structures, each with its own dialectic. It's what the waterfall dictates to me, with no logical link between us. Its descent sets me in motion." His partner responds, "Cerebral painting," and the first answers "action painting," and then repeats that in English.

This can at first seem like some sort of irrelevant parody of art criticism language, but there are two connections with the film and with Bresson. First, the suggestion of a kind of necessity in painting, as if the painter is dictated to by a multitude of structures each with their own dialectic, but with no logical link with the painter (no reason; these structures just "burst onto the canvas"), besides calling to mind Bresson's early career as a surrealist, also, with the denial of anything "cerebral," conforms to many of his strictures in the *Notes on the Cinematograph* book. It reminds us that his films too are not intentional representations of ideas, parts of a philosophical program that requires the form of the film. The form of the film is "dictated" by the meaning that emerges in the succession of images; it is not directed by the "cerebral" intentions of the filmmaker. Philosophical reflection is possible, just as attempts to explain what Pollock was up to are required, but whatever we come up with cannot be retrospectively attributed to the intentions of the filmmaker. Again, Bresson believes that the true "action" art, cinema, can make available to us a density of meaning and mattering in a world without a "cerebral" intention.

The second connection is the implicit suspicion about ex ante intentions in the arts (the cerebral) and in general, as the next conversation with two different tourists makes clear. One asks, "Can one be held responsible for a crime one commits involuntarily, but forgets out of nervous shock, or due to alcohol? The conscious gives way to the subconscious, even to the unconscious. The criminal may awaken unaware that he is a criminal." (At this point, Arnold, who has a great stake in the answer to this question, turns and looks at the conversants for a long time.) Neither party attempts an answer to the question, so a great deal is left hanging, since so much of what Bresson wants to show generally can be roughly said to be operating at the level of the subconscious or even the unconscious.

So, we have another expression of suspicion about the appeal to conscious intentions either in the explanation of action or in ascribing responsibility (or in accounting for the way a painting works). And this does seem connected not just to the Bressonian aesthetic but to the confusion we face in this film. It would be unfair to say of Marie, "She knew what she was getting into by joining Gérard and his gang, she bears responsibility for what happened to her." Her roadside meeting with Gérard, all at once a seduction, something of an assault, a consensual encounter, a childish teasing that goes wrong, an unknowing fall from innocence to experience (she can't possibly know what she is getting into), is not something that can be understood by working with the concept of her intentions. She can only know what she is getting into afterward; so what is her responsibility for "getting into it" beforehand? By withholding so much from us, Bresson presses on his viewers the need for interpretation under conditions of considerable ignorance, something that does not make the need any less pressing. It would be easy enough to say, in trying to understand why she is with Gérard, that at the back of her mind, Marie is always looking for someone who can help her leave the village, but we never quite know what we mean by "at the back of her mind."

Arnold has a last turn in the film when he suddenly inherits a fortune from a distant relative. The main consequence of this is a final face-off with his chief nemesis, Gérard, at a party Arnold throws for the whole town. Several things happen at Arnold's party, all as Balthazar looks on, a silent witness again. (Throughout we hear and see the sound of firecrackers, which scares Balthazar, causes him to jump in a way that foreshadows his being shot in the last scenes. Such a sequence of events helps connect Gérard's gang with the evil and indifference that will kill Balthazar.) Marie and her mother have it out over Gérard. When pressed by her, we can sense that Marie goes way over the top in expressing her love for him; in a wild exaggeration she says that she is even willing to kill herself for him (another ominous foreshadowing.) When her mother tells her that her behavior is killing her father, that he is suffering greatly, she replies with the air of truth that he loves his misery more than them, that he thrives on it. Her mother threatens to drag her home by force, but we know there is no chance of that happening. (Yet one more foreshadowing: when the older grain merchant intervenes during a dance to encourage Marie to go home, he is told that if he wants Marie, he will have to pay. This apparently gives Marie an idea.)

But the main event, one that frames the early part of the film and Gérard's gang's destruction of the automobiles, is a display of malevolent and especially meaningless destructive violence by Gérard. Knowing that Arnold will have to pay for the damages, he begins smashing everything in sight—large mirrors, scores of bottles—he turns over tables and creates general havoc (figure 4.11). As if to emphasize the absolute meaninglessness of this destruction, none of the other many partygoers even take notice, any notice *at all*, of Gérard's rampage. They continue to dance, as if sleepwalking, to a silly pop tune playing from the juke box. Such indifference is another feature of the general thoughtlessness that characterizes most of the village life. Nothing matters much—minimally just consumption, pleasure, money, power, sex. Aside from Marie's mother, no one cares much about, or even seems to understand, even to be aware of, love, friendship, solidarity. The suggestion is not that in Bresson's film world, such thoughtlessness should be contrasted with reflective or philosophical thoughtfulness, but by what is absent in the village, a sensitivity to some sense of sources of mattering in this world other than what is on the surface and commonly

FIGURE 4.11

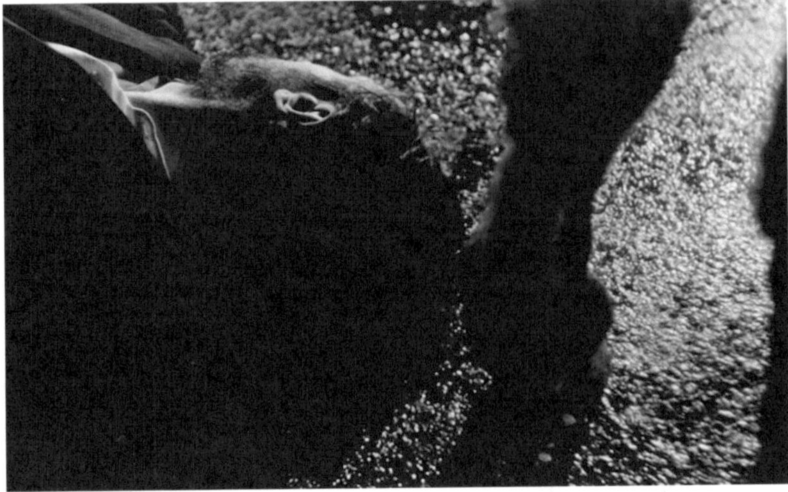

FIGURE 4.12

shared. Nothing better epitomizes the ways in which the meager sources of meaning available in the modern world require Bresson to film that world as he does than this display of meaningless destruction "as the band plays on" and no one cares.

As if to provide a bathetic ending to all this drama, Arnold is put on Balthazar and sent riding out of town, where, after saying an affectionate goodbye to a road marker and a utility pole (apparently in his mind his only friends), he expresses pity for them being stuck there watching the same fools pass by each day, and then falls off Balthazar and dies (figure 4.12).

The most disturbing scene occurs next. On a rainy night, the same night as the party, Marie shows up at the door of the grain merchant (played with malevolence by a philosopher friend of Bresson's, Pierre Klossowski), drenched from a storm. She tells him she cannot go home to her father, that she has broken with Gérard and his gang and she needs a place to sleep in his barn. (We see a brief shot of Balthazar in that barn, his ever-watchful face illuminated briefly by the rays of the lantern.) But it is immediately clear that something else is going on. She tells him, "You're so kind; if you want, I'll give you a kiss." She clearly has some plan in coming there. He does not respond but tells her to dry off and he will dry her clothes. She disrobes completely in front of him; he does not look away and throws her a large blanket. There then follows a brief exchange that makes clear the ethos, or we can say the summation of what matters, in the village world within which young people like Marie must find their way.

She tells him, "It's so ugly here; this is a place to die in." When he tells her he has no intention of dying, she asks if he believes in anything and he offers what might be a summary of the modern bourgeois world, not in its fantasy about itself, but as it is: "I believe in what I own. I love money, and I hate death."

Marie gets a jar of something to eat; he tries to take it away from her; she slaps his hand away. He puts a hand on her bare shoulder; she slaps it away for a second time. She comes to the apparent purpose of her visit and tells him it is known that he has gold and coins in the house. He gets a wad of bills, offers them to her, and she takes them. After a bit more of the merchant's views—the world is a marketplace; everything is for sale; honor is foolish—she gives the money back but says that what she really needs is a friend, someone to share with her pleasures and pain, and most significantly, a friend who can tell her how to get away. The merchant says he will be that friend but hopes there will be more pleasure than pain, and takes her, naked under the blanket and unresisting, onto his lap and the scene ends (figure 4.13).

In the next scene, she is buttoning her blouse in the barn with Balthazar. So, there is the usual Bressonian ellipsis, but given the obvious purpose of her visit, it seems that she has slept with the merchant in exchange for some unspecified help in leaving town, but we don't know for sure. All we really have learned is her desperation, her hatred for the village, and the merchant's summation of the world she so understandably wants to flee.

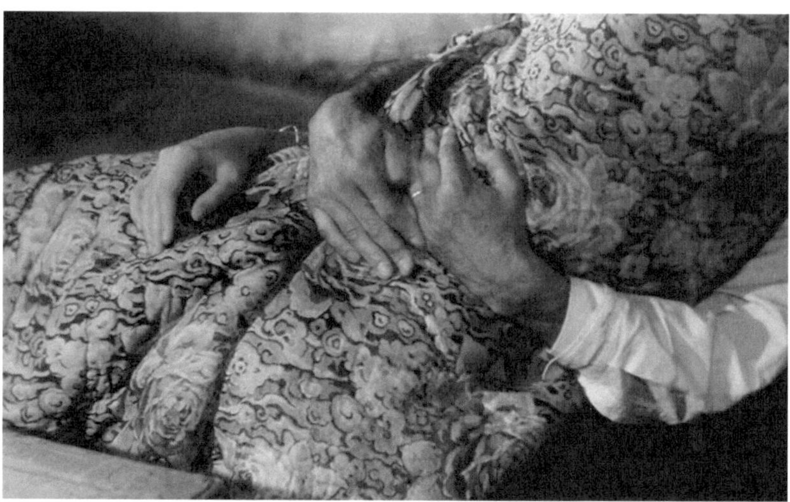

FIGURE 4.13

FIGURE 4.14

FIGURE 4.15

Another major ellipsis occurs when Jacques returns to attempt some reconciliation. Marie explains that it is too late, that he can never forgive her for what she has done. He asks what she has done, and then there is another ellipsis. We don't know how much she has confessed, either about Gérard, perhaps other boys in his gang, or about the merchant, but she thinks she is now ruined for a nice boy like Jacques. He tries to reassure her, but she tells him he bores her, that she has no more feelings, no tenderness. They are not, she says, in a world of make-believe but reality. This—Gérard, the merchant, her father's self-destructive pride, loving money and hating death—is reality. But when she goes to feed Balthazar she tells the donkey simply "I'll love him," as if her attachment to the world, her love, all that she feels she has lost, can be restored by an act of will. She tries to act on that resolve by insisting on confronting Gérard and his gang and telling them what she really thinks of them, clearly a dangerous idea.

She is stripped, beaten, and probably raped by the gang, and is found by her father and Jacques and carried home. Her mother later tells Jacques that Marie "is gone. She'll never be back."

The last scenes involve the gang's theft of Balthazar and their attempt to use him to smuggle consumer goods across the Spanish border. They are seen and shot at; Balthazar is hit, and we seem him the next morning still bleeding and dying. He heads down to a pasture and dies surrounded by the same animals, sheep, we heard when we first met him. The film thus leaves us with two startling images that complete the film's main contrast between Marie's world and Balthazar's animal world, and those images need no commentary (figures 4.14 and 4.15).

5
Mouchette's Mind

Mouchette begins with a very brief pre-credit prologue, a scene not in the Bernanos novel that serves as source material for the film.[1] Mouchette's mother, a presence more than a character in the film, appears alone in what appears to be an empty church. She only says two things: "What will become of them without me?" and "I can feel it in my breast, like a stone inside." She is dying of cancer, and, perhaps thinking of her three pregnancies,[2] notes that what is inside her now is not a child but a stone, a dead thing that is killing her. She does not pray or indicate any religious aspiration; she simply says these phrases, gets up and leaves as a passage from Monteverdi's 1610 *Magnificat* begins to play (figure 5.1). The credits then role over the empty chair she had been sitting on. The juxtaposition of her despair and this hymn is an exceedingly strange beginning to what is arguably the saddest of Bresson's films. The Virgin Mary's hymn of praise to God after learning of her fate seems hardly fitting. The first eight verses clash jarringly with what we are seeing and hearing in way that seems an almost bitter irony.

> *Magnificat anima mea Dominum.*
>
> My soul doth magnify the Lord.
> And my spirit hath rejoiced in God my savior.

1. There are quite a few divergences from the Bernanos novel, many more than in *Diary*. Bernanos only recounts the last twenty-four hours of Mouchette's life; Bresson extends the time to a week, two Sundays. He changes the location from Artois in the north to the Vaucluse region in the south, and he updates the time from the 1930s to the 1960s. Her relation with Arsène is also much altered, suppressed.

2. Since the *Magnificat* that we hear is a reference to Mary's response to the annunciation, her reference to the stone now inside her has a doubly ironic effect.

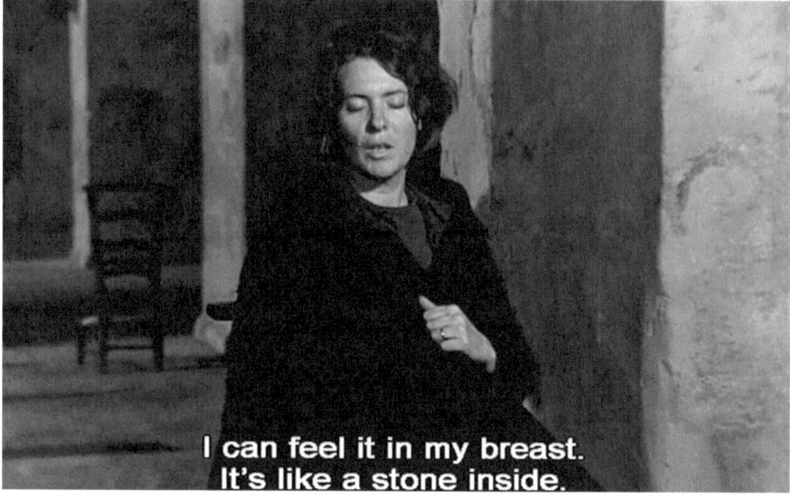

FIGURE 5.1

> For he regarded his handmaiden's lowliness;
> behold, henceforth all generations shall call me blessed.
> For he that is mighty hath magnified me: and holy is his name.
> And his mercy is on them that fear him: throughout all generations.
> He has shown strength with his arm; he hath scattered the proud in the imagination of their hearts.
> He hath put down the mighty from their seat: and hath exalted the humble.
> He hath filled the hungry with good things; and the rich he hath sent away empty.

The humble are clearly not exalted in the village we are about to see. This unusual opening, which Bresson added after the final filming, establishes a cinematic tone that foreshadows not just the hopelessness that pervades Mouchette's life, but the impossibility of imagining any such redemption from the pettiness and banality of the daily life we will see, and even the cruelty of any hope for the hungry and the humble.

In contrast with the view that the *Magnificat* functions like the references to religion in *Balthazar* (Gérard's pious singing in church and the impotence of the priest when Marie's father dies), that it "sounds" the irrelevance of any seventeenth-century piety, of any hope for redemption that will shadow the tone of the film thereafter, it is always possible to construct an alternate, contrasting reading. It is possible to see the contrast between the faith expressed in the *Magnificat* and the hopelessness and absence of grace in the film that follows as a measure of just what is required for faith, how hard it is to imagine an act of faith like Mary's when she is told what she is told, and how beautiful it is just because of its extreme difficulty. And it is true that in an interview with Yvonne Baby, Bresson himself tells us that the music "envelops the film in Christianity."[3] But, given the ambiguity of what it means for a film to be so enveloped, for a commentator to extract some aspiration for such a faith in a film that at every second suggests its impossibility not its difficulty strains credibility. This is especially so given the absence of any character or moment that could render such a leap at all credible. It seems more a measure of how intolerable many viewers find the cruelty and hopelessness of the atmosphere created in both *Balthazar* and *Mouchette* than any justified interpretation of what we see and hear. It is even possible to imagine a contrast between what Bresson actually shows us and what he might privately think what he shows us means or allows.[4]

The narrative proper begins with a scene in the woods surrounding the town that emphasizes two of the most prominent aspects of life in such a village: mutual surveillance among the citizens (together with the jealousy, resentment, and paranoia that follows such obsessive concern with others) and a cavalier, lax, even nihilistic approach to law or any rules of order, in favor of strategically successful self-servingness (or to make a leap, the ruthless logic of capitalism itself, a form of which is emerging in the village, signaled by the presence of the modern trucks constantly roaring by in the background). We see through dense foliage a man who we will soon learn is the local game warden, Matthieu (played by Jean Vimenet), as he watches intently (there are eight intense close-ups of his eyes moving back and forth in a stationary face, like a bird) a local poacher, Arsène (Jean-Claude Guilbert), who sets snares to catch birds. We learn very soon after these scenes that Mathieu is hardly the representative of law. His eagerness to catch Arsène is fueled by romantic jealousy and a bruised ego. But we learn all that later and have no clear idea what we are seeing or hearing in an intensified soundtrack. We then see, as Mathieu watches, a bird caught and struggling desperately in one of the snares, a dramatic but still unclear introduction to

3. Bresson (2013), 187. Note that he also says the music "is not about sustenance or reinforcement," leaving unclear what "envelops" could mean.

4. Typical of Bresson's studied ambiguity in what he says about his films is his remark about what he admires in the character Mouchette: "Her resistance to atrocity, the revelation that this child expects from death a thousand extraordinary just rewards." The phrase "a thousand extraordinary just rewards" suggests both an admiration for Mouchette's courage and a sadness at the pathos of such a hope. The former may explain why he says that her death is "not a cause for despair." Bresson (2013), 190.

the plight of Mouchette, a scene as hard to watch and listen to as the bird flaps its wings, struggling, as the actual history of Mouchette herself later. The image of a small bird, a partridge, struggling with a wire noose around its neck, entrapped, helpless, sets the tone for the story of Mouchette's fate, and Mouchette herself is often most at home in the fields and woods, nearly feral.[5] We see Arsène catch the bird and then, after a shot of his eyes (indicating he knows he is being watched), release the bird and walk off. (Arsène will have a role in Mouchette's suicide, which we will eventually experience as, however sad, a similar release from the miserable fate assigned to her.) As Mathieu returns home and complains to his wife that Aersène is again poaching, we see a very brief interposed scene of Mouchette (Nadine Nortier) at school with the other students, hesitating to enter the schoolhouse, and we then shift to another scene that introduces one of the two remaining plot elements (the other is Mouchette's home life): the local barmaid, Louisa (Marine Trichet), in some sort of triangular relation with both Arsène and Mathieu. The story of Mouchette, a story of a descent into suicidal despair, is thus embedded in the general picture of small-minded, petty, mutually surveilling village life, a competition between two men for the affections of Louisa (something everyone in town seems to know and gossip about), and her apparent manipulation of both men,[6] several indications of a lax moral and legal order, and an unimaginably miserable home life. We are introduced to Mouchette's father and brother as they deliver what is clearly contraband wine, hiding it from the suspicious police (who seem to realize what is going on but ignore it). As noted, in all the opening scenes of the film, there is no establishing dialogue or shots. We have no idea who any of these people are or what their connections are until well into the sequence of scenes, something typical of Bresson's use of synecdoche, ellipsis, and nonnarrative editing.

The village "world" of Mouchette, understood as some common attunement to what matters in life and what doesn't, is thus presented as having the narrowest possible horizon: vanity, egoism, suspicion, small-mindedness, and pettiness. As with *Au hasard, Balthazar*, this is not treated as a kind of common human sinfulness. Throughout the film, we see, or

5. "Mouchette's terror resembles the terror of a trapped animal." Bresson (2013), 185.

6. At one point she tells Arsène to go, to leave the bar, but as he leaves, she tells him, "but come back." At another, when Mathieu reminds her that she had promised him her affection, she tells him that that was the way she felt yesterday, but now she is not sure she will like him, that she would like to make him happy, but . . . Mathieu infers that she "loves someone else," an inference that increases his rage at Arsène. In the latter scene the leers on the faces of the other patrons make clear that everyone knows what is going on.

mostly hear, that the village is in transition.[7] The sound of heavy trucks in the background throughout indicates that the village is now on a major highway, and so its days as an isolated village are numbered. Mouchette's father, an oafish, mean-spirited, abusive drunk, daydreams like a child about a new truck to replace his dilapidated relic.[8] What we experience is something like a nineteenth-century village, from which the sustaining commitments of community, religion, politics, a sense of a common good, and familial love have all vanished, leaving only a kind of minimum individual commitment to money, sex, and status. Throughout it all, we constantly return to something that seems to shadow the whole film: the slow, painful death of Mouchette's mother, something only Mouchette seems concerned with. No neighbors ever come to visit or offer to help, no priest shows up, no one at Mouchette's school seems interested in her struggle as a young, fourteen-year-old girl thrust into the role of being the mother in a household with no help from her lout of a father or her brother, and especially no help with the small baby Mouchette must also care for.

This all contributes to an unusual psychological tone in the film. Typically in Bresson, his nonprofessionals do not "act," and there is minimal psychological expressiveness, only very rare "displays" of affection, frustration, anger; we infer such states from the actions we see, and for the most part we "see" enough to know what Mathieu is feeling, what Arsène thinks, that Louisa is enjoying playing both men off against each other, that Mouchette's classmates are self-centered and cruel. But the case of Mouchette is different. It is as if her inner life has been reduced to some degree near zero.[9] She often seems almost mindless, almost animal-like.[10] The lack of regard of anyone for her, her status as almost invisible to everyone, seems to have been internalized, as if her minimal status for everyone else has become

7. Jacob (1967) notices the emphasis in both *Au hasard, Balthazar* and *Mouchette* on rapid modernization in the villages, 52.

8. Lopate (1999) makes a correct and telling comment when he notes: "Bresson takes pains to show how deep are the roots of alcoholism in La France Profonde (far deeper than Catholicism), how surely the disease is passed on from father to son, how much harm it does to the women. Mouchette is, above all, a tragedy of alcoholism, only from the viewpoint of the nondrinking recipient rather than the lushes themselves: the father who beats her, the poacher who rapes her, the mother who guzzles gin to die, then moans her last words of advice to stay away from drunkards," 56.

9. The Bressonians, the Dardenne brothers, explore this theme with great sensitivity in their first feature film, *Rosetta*. See Pippin (2020b).

10. Rancière makes an interesting point about this: "Bernanos emphasized the gap between what was happening in Mouchette and how much of this she could understand. Bresson gave the girl's body a positive ability to use a synthesis of what happened to her for her own purposes," 28.

internalized, that she represents herself to herself as others do—as nothing. The village we soon see suffers from pathologies of misrecognition. Acknowledgment of status is either transactional and thus worthless (based on misrepresentation, lies, manipulation), granted only in fear of others not granting it, or withheld as a means of self-elevation. This last is what Mouchette suffers in such a dire way that her own self-sentiment seems affected. She often does not understand her own anger at her marginalization, and so the anger becomes generalized, its object nothing and everything.

This is one of the points where Bresson's mistrust of actorly expressiveness seems to me deeply tied to philosophical skepticism about the reliability of psychological explanation altogether, at least individualist psychological explanation,[11] a commitment itself tied to another about the inextricability of individual mindedness and the peculiarities of the social world in which such individuals find themselves. Such a social world is sustained by the commitments and attitudes of its participants, but those participants reflect a dependency on a horizon of possibilities and, especially in this case, a limitation on possibilities apparent in those commitments and attitudes. And, as I have been trying to show throughout, that social world is not presented as the perennial world of unavoidable human sinfulness, but a historical emerging social world of alienation, boredom, conformism, and materialism. Her father's dreams of a better truck, the trucks rushing by frequently in the background, the assumptions about law and morality, the anxious mutual surveillance and suspicion, all have a historical inflection. This is a world of modern carnivals with mixing social classes in contrast with remnants of an old world where higher classes (whom we do not see until the end of the film) still have hunting privileges denied to others. It is the burden of this world on a confused and isolated Mouchette that crushes her spirit.[12]

There are several examples of her unusual and minimal mental life and its origins. One is her treatment in school. Mouchette is clearly the poorest girl

11. See Bresson on *Mouchette* and "my distrust of analysis and psychology." Bresson (2013), 187.

12. So I disagree with comments like those of McNeese (1991) when she says, "Filmmakers such as Truffaut and Godard sought to effect a sense of spontaneity to give expression to a young and spirited generation growing up in a rapidly changing capitalist society. Bresson, by contrast, has attempted to divert viewers from the very distractions in modern culture that offer the illusion of freedom," 267. She is right about the suspicion of spontaneity and the illusion of freedom, but there is no diversion—just the contrary. I think he is also suspicious of attributing any new sort of spontaneity and rebellion in youth. In *The Devil, Probably* and *L'Argent* he is both invoking the trope of disaffected, rebellious youth and suspicious of it.

in the all-girl class. Her clothes are little better than rags, and she must wear her brother's hand-me-down clogs, which must be at least two sizes too large, and which noisily announce her entrance wherever she goes, making sounds that she seems to want to accentuate, as if stomping with them in a sign of defiance (as when she enters the schoolroom). *Mouchette* represents Bresson's most sophisticated use of sound. The clogs, the truck noises, the motorbikes, the gunshots, the crash of bumper cars, Mouchette's singing voice, the rain, the birds fluttering, the fire crackling, the baby crying, the church bells in the background, a tractor noise in the distance, all become an integral part of the narration itself, bear as much thematic and atmospheric weight as the images and their sequences. They effectively "establish the density of a rural world."[13] All of these sounds are intensified, sometimes artificially, louder on the soundtrack than they would be in a normal realist film, and often by contrast with silences, especially the sullen silences in the social world, as the villagers slurp their drinks in silence. In other words, the concentration on the sounds allows them to emerge as a component of the film that *means* something: entrapment, hostility, routine, boredom, a thinglike materialism that reflects the social world as much as what the natural world has become in such a time (to be owned, policed, hunted).

Her teacher is a frightening harridan who singles Mouchette out for humiliation when she at first refuses to sing, then cannot hit the right note (B-flat) in the song the class is singing.[14] (This is perhaps a small moment of unconscious rebellion by Mouchette since we learn later in a decisive scene with Arsène that she can certainly sing the whole song perfectly well, and she has a lovely voice.) In a rare moment of explicit expressiveness, the humiliation in front of the class brings Mouchette to quiet tears. (The teacher had gone so far as to press Mouchette's face into the keyboard to sound the correct note [figure 5.2].) In a much more explicit act of rebellion, when school is dismissed, Mouchette runs off a slope of the road and throws several dirt clods at her schoolmates, who react impassively, as if they are used to Mouchette and, again, treat her as nearly nonexistent, not even worth getting angry at. There seems to be no point to the attack, no

13. Michelson (1968), 318. Hanlon's (1998) comment sums it up very well. "Sound is Bresson's most important source of narrative economy, never duplicating an image's message. Sound may even be substituted for that image. The exchange of sound for image relieves Bresson's films of the redundancy of conventional sound realism and frees sound for use as an emblem," 307.

14. The song, a poem by Casimir Delavigne set to music, *Aux Americains*, is an attempt by Columbus to counter the despair of his men by encouraging them to have hope: give him three more days and he will show them a whole new world. Hope for a better future, a new world, is exactly what Mouchette is not allowed to have.

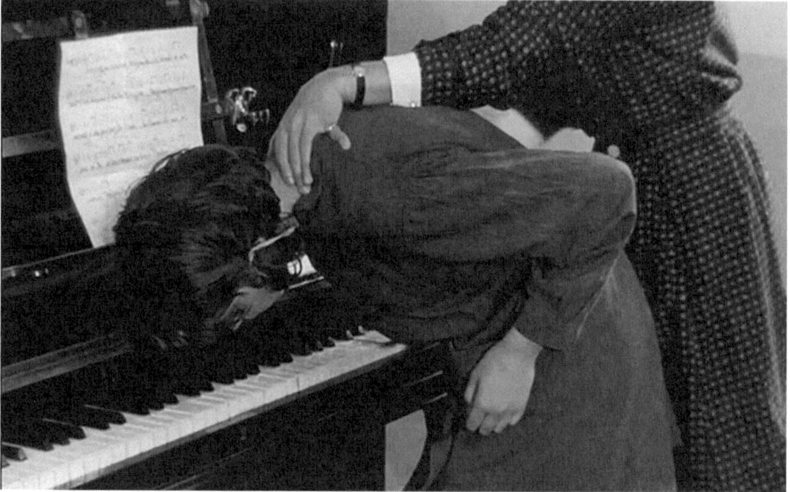

FIGURE 5.2

purpose other than a lashing out that does not seem "minded" and thus purposeful in any determinate way. This is a strange state, characteristic often of Marie in *Balthazar*, but in her to a lesser, or less radical degree. (Both Marie and Mouchette lose their virginity by violence and are consumed with shame and self-hatred, although both had experienced some strange and confused affection for their rapists.) Bernanos refers to Mouchette's "reduced" consciousness, one might call it, several times in the novel: "At first, Mouchette would not recognize her own voice [when being forced to sing]" (10); "For years, Mouchette had felt herself a stranger amongst the villagers, dark and hairy like goats, whom she hated so much" (30); "Any sort of reflection was so unusual for her that she was unaware of the enormous effort she was making to understand. By dreaming, she often managed to escape from herself, but it was a long time since she had lost the secret of those mysterious ways by which one entered into oneself" (33); "She had never before had time for any introspection" (54); "It [her rape by Arsène] had no beginning and no end, it was more like a confused noise in her head, a kind of funeral hymn" (60); "She seemed absorbed in thought, but in fact her mind was completely empty" (87). This is not a state peculiar to Mouchette in the village, just much more extreme because of her near complete loneliness.[15] She has that animal-like, feral status, but she is

15. In the novel, Mouchette's father is said to be a silent man, not "from ill-will or from avarice but from a kind of stupid stubbornness, which took the place of thought, which he took for thought," 70.

certainly not wholly animal. While she speaks fewer lines than any central character in all of Bresson's films, she is not wholly passive, has and shows her contempt for the adults, challenges them, often mutely and physically but still passionately.

Charles Barr characterizes this situation as like *Diary* (and Victorian literature) as a "dialectic between involvement with the world and withdrawal from it," and in both cases, although quite different in tone, withdrawal wins out, in this case in suicide. This should not though be seen as an individual decision or pathology and should rather be taken as a comment on the fragility and contingency of the ways in which the world comes to matter and fails to matter, or the way in which a world, a horizon of possible mattering at a time, can or cannot elicit what Heidegger calls the fundamental human orientation to anything in the world, "care," *Sorge*, a practical comportment that is not itself based on but a ground of beliefs and attitudes about importance. Mouchette is not a mere individual neurotic, the product of mistreatment by her parents, although she certainly is a victim of that. It is the world, this village world, that has failed her, and which only sustains others because of their collective and thus mutually sustaining investment in the narrowness of care about money, self-satisfaction, and status, all that is available as sources of meaning. (Lest we think this is all just an indictment of small-minded village life at the time, we shall see the same phenomenon in the urban setting that characterizes his later films.)

In a bizarre end of the school scene (not in the novel), several girls, when boys ride by on their motorbikes (as in *Balthazar*, another image of the new pace, speed, modernization of the village), mount some gym bars and flip over, revealing, clearly *displaying*, their panties (figure 5.3). The consciousness of this emerging, inchoate, and coarse sense of sexuality, as with the boys who reveal themselves and taunt Mouchette, is in contrast to the unknowingness so extreme in Mouchette that it cannot even be described as innocence, in the way it would not be quite correct to describe animals as "innocent."

To emphasize the isolation of Mouchette in this regard, and the danger to her of this unknowingness, Bresson shows us Mouchette the next morning half-dressed in her slip, making coffee for the family, making clear to the viewer that she already has the body of a young woman, although there is never any indication that her mother has yet explained to her the implications of this status.[16] (We know very little of the relationship be-

16. In a feeble attempt at a correction for this negligence later, right before she dies, she warns Mouchette about taking up with idlers and drinkers.

FIGURE 5.3

tween Mouchette and her mother, except that there was never much of one. We are told in the novel that "her mother had never been affectionate and Mouchette had never received caresses from her hands" [120]. And that Mouchette "had never known the sweetness of a real caress. Only once perhaps." This was from a stranger, a "big fair-haired girl" who had bumped into her and caressed her cheek, all of which "gave her a strange rebellion against tenderness which made her so solitary" [122].)

The villagers gather at the bar where Louisa works before and after Sunday church. In fact, Sunday church seems merely the occasion for the gathering at the bar, and we see Mouchette again, as with the dirt throwing, expressing her general state of rebellion in a way that seems nonstrategic, again barely "minded" in a purposeful way. We see that she does have "dress shoes," not the oversized clogs, likely reserved exclusively for church, and she stomps with them through a mud puddle, dirtying them and provoking a vicious shove from her father in punishment.

There is some sort of fair in town, and Bresson shows us several more dimensions of village life. First, Mouchette works Sundays at the bar, helping wash up, and promptly turning over the money to her father, who will no doubt proceed to drink it away. Second, in a sign that Mouchette's miserable status is well known in the village, a woman with a small baby, seeing Mouchette gazing at the bumper car ride, silently buys her a token so she can ride herself. This is the only act of kindness shown to Mouchette in the film, and it produces the only moment of joy, or at least a smile, for Mouchette. (The scene is poignant in the way the motorcycle ride is in *Diary*—as if

FIGURE 5.4

to remind Mouchette of what she is missing right before she goes back to missing it, an escape from her agonizing loneliness.)[17] She begins to bump cars with a young boy about her own age, in the manner of teenagers, a way of establishing a connection, which he responds to, smiles back (figure 5.4). She even follows him after the ride is over; he gives her encouraging glances over his shoulder, and they end up together at a shooting gallery. But before they can speak, her father arrives, slaps her hard twice and shoves her away, all without saying a word or explaining his anger. Presumably, he wants no distractions that would keep her from taking care of him and the household. The fair scene also ends with a bizarre exhibition of Louisa's preference for Arsène. The two of them ride a flying capsule ride, and Mathieu must look on forlornly as they circle far above him, as if taunting him. It seems a kind of childhood regression to essentially high school behavior, and the sight of the two of them is certainly infantilizing, but this sets up the two men for a nearly deadly encounter later during the same storm in the woods when Mouchette is raped, and for a while we believe that Arsène may have killed Mathieu in their struggle. The villagers goad Mathieu about the situation, telling him he is being made a fool of, further fueling the fires of jealousy. (In spite of all the tension among the three of them, there seems not a flicker of real passion, certainly nothing romantic, just a sort of grudging, mean

17. Pipolo's (2010) formulation is apt: "It is one of the occasional revelations that makes us aware of the spirit of life that has been crushed," 225.

competition for possession and status, all of it taking place as if both under the gaze of the whole town and aware of it taking place under that gaze, as if that is the point.)

As Mouchette leaves school, after another episode of dirt throwing, being ignored and the girls riding away on boys' motorbikes, a storm is brewing as she walks home through the woods. This begins the core of the film, a twenty-minute continuous sequence in which whatever little stability and order there is in Mouchette's life falls apart. In her exchanges with Arsène, we finally hear her speak, converse, realize that she is an intelligent girl who wants, as badly as Marie, some solace and comfort from someone and she will take it where she can get it. The heavy thunderstorm hits, she is drenched and seeks shelter under a tree to wait out the rain, which does not let up. Finally, she attempts to begin her journey again, but the ground is now mud, and she loses one of her clogs and comes upon a renewal of the Mathieu-Arsène pas de deux. Mathieu discovers Arsène setting a large trap, and they quarrel and come to blows. As the fight gets serious with Arsène choking Mathieu and the latter biting Arsène's hand, their wrestling stops, and they both start chuckling and drinking Arsène's flask of booze, suddenly as if the best of friends. They split up and Arsène comes across Mouchette just as she is rolling up her tights high onto her leg. Bresson has eliminated from the film all the reference in the novel to Mouchette's earlier naive but genuine interest in Arsène, who seems in Bernanos to be a much younger man and attractive (mention is made of his bronze chest). We have seen the state Bresson is interested in with Marie in *Balthazar*, alternating between fear and even revulsion, on the one hand (with Gérard), and sexual attraction and fascination, on the other. That theme is much more subtly treated in the violent scene that follows in *Mouchette*, but as we shall see, it is an unmistakable aspect of Bresson's exploration of the difficult issue of what all of this, as it comes at her now rapidly and violently, "means" for Mouchette, all again on the assumption that pinning down a determinate characterization of her mind is likely hopeless.

Arsène at this point (things change as he drinks more) is solicitous of Mouchette and offers to help her find her clog. He takes her to a hut where there is a fire, they can dry out, and he can refill his flask. They both drink, Mouchette probably already far more than she is used to. While Arsène is out, Mouchette hears two shots; she looks over and sees that Arsène has not brought his rifle, but the shots are the basis of a story that prompts Arsène to believe that he needs an alibi, that he may have killed Mathieu. Arsène rehearses the story he wants Mouchette to tell and begins trying to erase all traces that they were in the hut. (We don't exactly know what he has in mind, or what happened when he was out.) They leave the hut, try

FIGURE 5.5

for another hideout at one of Arsène's friends, and are apparently rebuffed. But Arsène tells her that he has another way of managing. They go to some sort of shed, Arsène builds a large fire (he wants lots of ashes as evidence that they were there all night and explains the new alibi to Mouchette, who by now has begun to assume a warier countenance, clearly uneasy and suspicious [figure 5.5]).

Arsène tells Mouchette he may have killed Mathieu, but as he tries to explain, the beginning of what will be an epileptic fit begins to come over him. As he explains why he thought Mathieu might be dead, Mouchette makes her longest speech in the film. It is the one indication of that affection for Arsène that Bernanos makes more of. She clearly regards the poacher and herself as the village outcasts and so as having a bond; she feels she must protect him. The fit intensifies; Arsène falls and writhes on the floor as Mouchette gently lifts and holds his head until it subsides. She smiles gently at him, wipes his face, and even softly sings, perfectly this time, the school song, Columbus's attempt to encourage hope. After she tells him she is completely loyal and would rather die than hurt him, Arsène, who had been preparing to leave, now seems aroused, and within seconds Mouchette realizes something of what is going on and pushes him away. He seems to hunt her like prey in the cabin and eventually catches her under a table on all fours, crouching like an animal, and he throws her down. There is no question that this is now a violent rape of a fourteen-year-old girl and that she is terrified (figure 5.6). But there is also no question that, despite the difficulty of understanding what all this must be like for Mouchette,

FIGURE 5.6

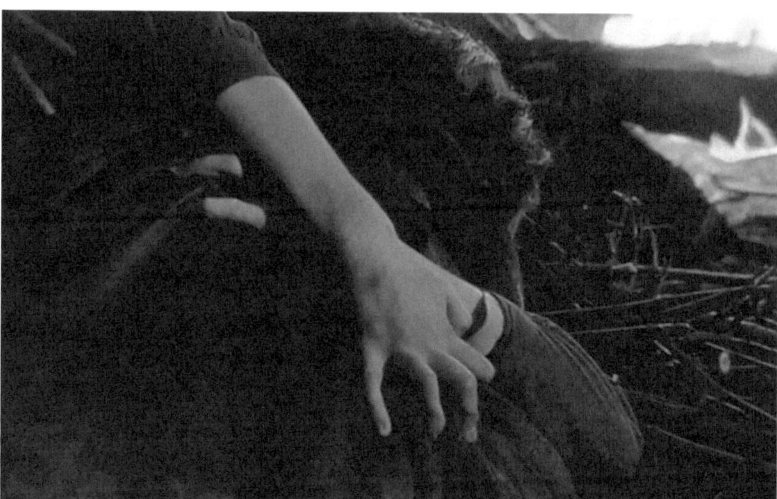

FIGURE 5.7

it is also the case that her loneliness has reached such desperate proportions that someone desiring her, even this drunk rapist, means something important to her and she ends up wrapping her arms around Arsène and embracing him (figure 5.7).

Mouchette returns home in the early morning to find her mother all alone with a baby she cannot care for (the husband and son are "out"), and Mouchette must immediately assume her maternal duties, but she also badly needs someone to talk with about what has happened to her. She's weeping throughout her ministrations, and she wakes up crying. She tries to talk with her mother, but the baby interrupts and then her mother wants some gin to help with the pain. By the time Mouchette is ready and informs her mother that she has to tell her something, her mother has died.

Her mother's death begins the final spiral into complete hopelessness, although it is almost correct to say, as paradoxical as it is, that Mouchette begins to despair utterly without having the resources to know what is happening to her, that she is in a state of despair. She is clearly sad and knows that she is sad, and clearly furious, and knows that she is, but her self-awareness cannot extend further than that. The first sign of her anger and bitterness is when she leaves to get milk for the baby, and her father tells her to stop staring at him, calls her a little hussy. She spits out *merde*, shit, and leaves.

As she walks to get the milk, she is called into the grocer's for some coffee, and while we might think she will finally experience some comfort and solace for her mother's death, we know enough about the village to suspect that the owner and a customer only want to pump her for gossip, which we have learned seems to be the main topic of conversation in the village. Sure enough, when the top button of Mouchette's smock falls open, the women can see a large scratch on her chest, and they immediately (and rather inexplicably) infer some sexual escapade, calling her a little slut, without knowing anything of what has happened to her. One would think that the women would want to know who hurt her, who did this to her. She sees in their eyes their disgust with her, spills the coffee she had been given, tosses the croissant back, and storms off.

Still confused about the night before, Mouchette wanders by Mathieu's place, no doubt to verify that he was really killed, and is astonished to see him alive and uninjured. He calls her in and interrogates her, discovers she spent the night in Arsène's cabin. His wife intervenes and is more gentle with Mouchette, realizing that Arsène had given her gin and probably raped her. But in response to this sympathy (and implicit criticism of Arsène), Mouchette, in an act of pathetic "loyalty" to her rapist, blurts out that Arsène is her lover and runs from the house.

She walks back through the town, still with no milk, and is called into the house of an old woman. We learn in the novel that she is a former servant of the Marquis de Champains and for many years has served as *veilleuse*, an old woman who attends to the dead, sits by the corpse, simply watches it. She offers Mouchette a shroud for the body, and some old dresses for herself. She tells the wary and suspicious Mouchette that she loves the dead, that she understands them. As Mouchette listens, she engages in another act of rather formless rebellion against the town. She grinds her muddy feet into the carpet, staining it, and she whispers, "You disgusting old thing."

Mouchette cuts across a field and a scene begins that lets us know we are coming full circle from the beginning of the film. The film began with the suffering of small animals and its penultimate scene is the same, this time, in a clear reference to Renoir's *Rules of the Game*, with hunters we have never seen before (obviously from the social class allowed to hunt on these fields) shooting rabbits as Mouchette watches.[18] We see and hear more than a dozen shots, and cut to frightened rabbits running, until one is shot and dies in some agony before us. It is as if the old woman has raised the question of death for Mouchette, and in a way that almost affirms it, and we then see the fate of weak and powerless creatures, unable to escape those with no regard for their lives. Mouchette's mother has died, she is now completely alone, she has been raped and it is clear that the village will blame her, and what she sees around her is the slaughter of small animals.

The suicide of a child is among the most painful scenes a viewer can be asked to watch, but in this case the tonality or atmosphere of the scene is at first oddly playful. Mouchette has put on one of the dresses given to her (torn it, indifferently), and, sitting on the bank of an old quarry now filled with water, rolls down to its edge. She stops well short of the water, and sees someone passing by, a farmer on a tractor. In a final gesture, attempting some contact with someone, as if she could get some acknowledgment of her existence, what she is vaguely thinking of doing might be avoided (figure 5.8). The farmer turns, sees her, but ignores her.

On the second roll down the bank, she gets much closer to the water, stopped only by a few branches from going in. On the third, the camera first stays on the last spot on the bank that we see, and we hear her hit the water. Then we see her white form under the water, but there is no struggle, no resistance to the water filling her lungs. The scene is peaceful, and we hear the *Magnificat* playing again (figure 5.9).

As usual with Bresson, the suicide scene is preceded by no deliberation, voice-over, conversation with another, any expression of agonized

18. This is not the only dimension of the reference to Renoir. See Rancière (2014), "Also lifted from Renoir is the 'professional' and love rivalry between the gamekeeper Schumacher and the poacher Marceau, which is projected onto the gamekeeper Mathieu and the poacher Arsène. So the plot changes direction. Bernanos's narrative was wholly focused on Mouchette whose path to the cross he followed stage by stage. Bresson makes Mouchette a helpless hostage ensnared in the rivalry between the gamekeeper and the poacher for the favours of the barmaid (whose existence only gets a single passing mention in the novel)," 25.

FIGURE 5.8

FIGURE 5.9

uncertainty or other clear indication of motivation. The scene looks back to Marie's sudden and unexplained "disappearance" from *Au hasard, Balthazar,* very likely another post-rape suicide but with no insight into Marie herself, and forward to *The Devil, Probably*, where the grossly incompetent psychiatrist suggests to Charles the Roman solution to not having the nerve to kill oneself (ask a friend to do it), just as the *veilleuse* praises the comforts

PLATE 1

PLATE 2

PLATE 3

PLATE 4

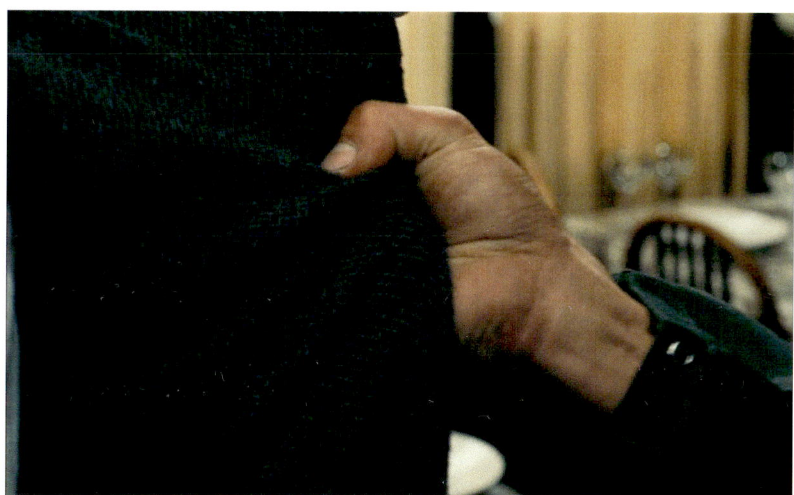

PLATE 5

PLATE 6

PLATE 7

PLATE 8

PLATE 9

PLATE 10

PLATE 11

PLATE 12

PLATE 13

PLATE 14

PLATE 15

and beauty of death to Mouchette.[19] And just as when it is unclear whether Charles will go through with it or not, he is suddenly shot from behind by his friend, Mouchette seems to play at rolling down the hill until we suddenly realize that she is preparing to drown herself. Bernanos comments on the suicide in a frequently cited passage:

> People generally think of suicide as an act like any other, the last link in a chain of reflections, or at least of mental images, the conclusion of a supreme debate between the instinct to live and another, more mysterious instinct of renouncement and refusal. But it is not like that. Apart from certain abnormal exceptions, suicide is an inexplicable and frighteningly sudden event, rather like the kind of chemical decompositions which currently-fashionable science can only explain with absurd or contradictory hypotheses. (Bernanos 2016, 119)

In Bresson's treatment, it would be more correct to say that the event is not psychologically explicable in the terms of normal individual motivation, and "explicable" is a term freighted with notions of causality. The suggestion here is that Bresson is trying to make the event understandable, meaningful even, by showing us it within the context of the village world Mouchette finds herself in. "Showing" is the key notion; all the details of the village life and the way they are photographed, the poaching, smuggling, gossip, mean-spiritedness, selfishness, and basic worthlessness of village life build up into a context where suicide seems like the final act of resistance from Mouchette, the "conclusion" of throwing dirt, stomping in a puddle, spitting out *merde*, tossing a croissant, grinding mud into the carpet, whispering "disgusting old thing," and defiantly calling Arsène her "lover." This buildup is like how chemical decomposition is accurate by contrast with willfulness, but only roughly like it. It is a result of sorts, but of the slow but inexorable dissolving of care, concern with life in such a world. There is very little we are shown worth caring about in such a world, even though Mouchette's last wave at the farmer on the tractor indicates a very slim thread of possible hope—denied when he looks away.

It is understandable that many commentators see this moment as something like an escape from the earthly veil of tears. Pipolo tells us that

19. In the novel, where we do hear more of Mouchette through indirect discourse, after talking with the old woman, Mouchette is said to remember "of what the old woman has said was one thing, 'death.' She seemed to have heard the word for the first time." Bernanos (2006), 118.

Mouchette's act "though suicide . . . is also life-enhancing." Charles Barr also tells us that the act "is a physical, accepting act, and though it is a suicide it is life-enhancing in a manner characteristic of Rossellini." (He refers to *Europe 51* and *Germany Year Zero*, both of which involve the suicides of children.) And Michael Estève, in an article comparing Bresson's treatment with Bernanos's in the novel, tells us that "the suicide of Mouchette affirms itself, beyond despair and the temptation of Satan, as a quest for super-terrestrial value that would alone be capable of making one attain another life."

Mouchette's life has become so miserable that of course in some sense or other, her death is indeed a liberation, but "life-enhancing"? Yes, she is free from her father, the cruelty of her classmates, the hostility and selfishness of the villagers, and like Balthazar's death, the film creates an aura of peaceful release from suffering in the way it is staged. But what life is enhanced, unless the commentators mean eternal life? But if that is so, how can it be that suicide is considered one of the gravest if not the gravest of sins?

6
Counterfeit Life in *L'Argent*

L'Argent is adapted from a rambling Tolstoy short story, "Faux Billets," which has, at least in its part 1, the same basic plot. An attempt by an entitled youth to pass off a counterfeit bill begins a chain of consequences for many unconnected people that finally ends with vicious murders. Bresson combines two characters from the story in his Yvon Targe, played by a young architect Bresson knew, Christian Patey, and he leaves out part 2, where Tolstoy shows us the murderer attacked by conscience and confessing, and which purports to show that just as an evil deed can spread like a contagion, so can good, or for Tolstoy love, and it can repair some of the damage. There is none of that in Bresson, although we shall have to consider the meaning of Yvon's turning himself in to the police in the film's closing shots.[1]

In each of Bresson's thirteen films, the titles announce a focus on individuals. There are Angels of Sin; Ladies of the Bois de Boulogne; the country priest; the man who escaped; the pickpocket; Joan of Arc; Balthazar; Mouchette; the gentle woman; the dreamer (of *Four Nights of a Dreamer*); Lancelot of the Lake; the Devil (perhaps the first expression of skepticism that what drives action in the films is not so much an individual agent); and now we have as the main "character," L'Argent. The contrast immediately puts into question the status of individual subjectivity, one could even say the ownership of one's own mind, in a world where the main "actor" is money.

1. See Moravia (1998). "In *L'Argent*, Bresson has left 'good,' that is, Tolstoy's view of 'good' in the shadows, in order to concentrate on 'evil' and to undertake a precise and impersonal study of the way in which the inevitable social secretion is formed" (407).

The film is structured in several ways. There are eight characters in a plot and a mirroring subplot. The main plot involves Yvon Targe, a young working-class man who drives for a heating oil company. It is Yvon whose life is ruined by the false bills. He accepts them in payment, is told later that day by a waiter that they are false and is arrested. The shop owners and their assistant who knowingly passed the false bill to Yvon shamelessly lie to the police and in court (they claim not even to recognize Yvon), but they agree to drop the charges, and Yvon's case is dismissed. However, he cannot return to his old job because of the arrest, has a wife and child to care for but cannot find work. (Yvon has signed receipts from the shop owners, but in his bewilderment that they refuse to acknowledge that they even recognize him, he does not defend himself. Unaccustomed to the social class he finds himself in, confused, he simply finds the whole situation "crazy.") Unemployed, desperate, with a family to feed, he accepts a role as a getaway driver in a bank robbery that goes wrong. Arrested again he receives three years in prison. While he is in prison his young daughter dies of diphtheria, his wife leaves him, and he attempts suicide. When released, he checks into a hotel, and we are totally unprepared for the fact that he suddenly murders and robs the two innkeepers. He comes across an older woman in that town, whom we later learn is a widow full of charity, forgiveness, and generosity. She knows Yvon is the murderer but feeds and shelters him, after which he murders her and her father, daughter, son-in-law, grandson, and the family dog. Shortly thereafter, he comes across a number of police in a café and suddenly confesses to them.

The mirroring and sometimes comic subplot concerns the photo shop where the false bills were passed to Yvon. It is a mirroring subplot because the two narratives tell the story of the descent into crime by two young men—one occasioned by gross mistreatment and injustice; the other, Lucien, the shop assistant who denied ever seeing Yvon, by the realization that no one in this world abides by any rules they can get away with breaking—a psychological disintegration and a moral one. Yvon had received the counterfeit bills from Lucien, and later when the police arrive with Yvon, Lucien, who had been taken aside and clearly coached by the shop owner (who had promised his wife that he would pass on the bills) does his bidding and baldly lies about ever having seen Yvon before. But he assumes that the shop owner, by encouraging the lies, has conceded that we are all out only for ourselves, and so Lucien promptly tries to steal money from the shop by inflating camera prices and pocketing the difference. He is quickly discovered and fired, and he too begins a life of crime, robbing ATM machines and later the shop owners' own safe. He is arrested and meets Yvon again in prison, where he attempts to apologize and offers him a spot in an escape attempt. The attempt fails and Lucien is sent off to a higher security prison.

The other structuring elements are plot points, three apparent chapters: Yvon before prison; the three years in prison; and the last twenty minutes or so at the kindly widow's home. This structure shows us another formal closure centered on dysfunctional families; the film opens with one, what appears to be a wholly transactional, loveless family, and closes with the widow's family, where she is oppressed by a tyrannical father and must toil away for her unappreciative relatives. (In the middle as it were we have Yvon's, which appears to be a loving and happy family until it is all taken from him by a calamitous chance event motivated by money.)

But it is the visual style and how it reflects Bresson's view on the primary availability of a meaningful world in experience that accounts for the real formal structure of the film. Its opening credits begin with a mysterious shot of an ATM machine's door closing and the sound of Parisian traffic rushing by. (The shot is a tight one, with no identifying signs, so at first viewing it is not quite possible to realize what we are seeing.) We see the door closing, but not opening, suggesting right away the divisions we see in the film: those who have access to money, who can open the door; those who do not; and those who steal it. (The suggestion of a prison peephole is also clearly deliberate.) We hear a stream of traffic as we read the title, which seems to suggest that this energetic rush is all fueled by what the word we are reading, *L'Argent*, designates.[2] And by placing the title over the reference to Tolstoy's title, "faux billets," we already have an indication that money does not need to be counterfeited to be false; money fuels a form of life that is itself false, based on a form of human connectedness that is not connectedness (plate 1). (It is a false life in the sense of Adorno's famous phrase from *Minima Moralia*, that one cannot live rightly in a false life, or even that in our world, "life does not live.") Money is not symbolic in the film, any more than the material and conditioned quality of our lives is a symbol for anything else. It simply *is* that aspect of our current finitude, the economically, bodily, contingent materiality that we experience as an unchosen fate, the unavoidable horizon for what cannot but matter, and which has always inspired the counter-idea of transcendence, that ideal that so many look for sometimes so desperately in Bresson. The most powerful life-defining material element in the late modern world is money, and while Bresson's film

2. See Pipolo (2010), 340.

depicts the abnormal in the destruction of the soul of one human being, that exaggeration illuminates a feature of existence that is also captured by Bresson's frequent invocation of prison life. Actual prisons figure in several films—*Angels of Sin, A Man Escaped, Pickpocket, The Trial of Joan of Arc, L'Argent*—but as many have pointed out, prison seems also a kind of ontological metaphor for any possible mode of being in the twentieth century, a metaphor for a distinct kind of unfreedom. That some aspects of what might matter in human life, what makes a life a distinctly human life, cannot matter in such a world is that kind of unfreedom, an extreme restriction in what would otherwise be possible.

The opening minutes of the film introduce another implication of the "visible god": class. A member of an upper-class *haut bourgeois* family passes off the false bill to middle-class shopkeepers who pass it off to a working-class man and, as it is said, the buck then stops with him. Although, as I have suggested, Bresson works to eliminate any sort of directed response to the viewer, his very minimalism allows something like the essential sources of significance in the common world they inhabit to emerge, and some sense of disgust at what we see of and pity for Yvon are unavoidable, however stripped down the emotional tonality and, paradoxically, however gruesome the many murders. As I have been suggesting, I don't believe the minimalism of the scene staging, the general atmosphere of what seems very low intensity existence, even arid and lifeless, is connected wholly to Bresson's efforts to avoid theatricality by means of new cinematographic techniques. The psychological atmosphere created by the minimalism creates the impression of a general human indifference to each and something like a weak or fragile commitment to the requirements of the world within which they live. In this film more than any others, we see more clearly that this is not meant to be a feature of human life as such, but *this* sort of life, a distinctive historical world that in this film even has a name, L'Argent.[3] What that world requires is not just money but the entire culture that fuels its acquisition—competition, self-interest, mistrust, false dealing, self-protection, wariness, status, humiliation—and at various moments in

3. Cf. Jones (1999). "Bresson's strategy throughout *L'Argent* is not to cultivate or dramatize the abnormality or psychosis buried within society. Rather, he allows society to reflect back on itself, to give a moral accounting of itself. If an employer pays his assistant off for lying in court, the assistant will take the hint and steal from the employer; if a man has his livelihood taken away from him, he's going to resort to making money illegally. The tome isn't pedantic. It's elemental."

the film, we cannot but be repulsed by all this, or at least Bresson seems clearly to be expressing his repulsion.[4]

For example, we learn everything we need to know about the original bill-passer's wealthy family, Norbert's family, in the first few minutes of the film. As with the ATM door, doors opening and especially closing, a favorite trope of Bresson, begin creating the sense of human disconnectedness that keeps reappearing throughout the film. (And I don't mean that the images suggest the idea of disconnectedness, as if we are to discursively decode what we see; we are coming to understand something about the worldly aspects of their existence, a kind of closed-off-ness to others, even if we never formulate it into an idea. And as an aside, I want to suggest again that this is the main philosophical achievement of Bresson's work, that the world is only available because of its nondiscursive intelligibility, its presence in our experience of the film.) The desk, the clothes, the attitudes in the looks, all let us sense immediately what matters to these people (and hence something about the worldly environment in which it could matter) even if it would be far too simple to say that what matters is simply money and the status and power it bestows. The fundamentality of money in such a world affects everything else that could matter (plate 2).

Norbert owes some money at school, and neither his father nor his mother will advance him anything from his allowance. He calls on a friend, Martial, for help. Martial shows him what they both clearly think is an excellent counterfeit bill of large denomination (it isn't and is easily spotted by anyone with experience), and Martial promises to help him pass it. His target is a local photo shop where they will buy a cheap frame, pass the bill, and keep the change. But as they prepare to leave, without saying anything, Martial takes a photo album out of a desk and shows it to Norbert and Norbert leafs through it. It is an album of photos of artworks, all female nudes. Their only dialogue about this is Martial remarking that the human body is beautiful. This of course raises the question of why Bresson would include such a strange scene, which appears to be an irrelevant display of teenage

4. Price (2011) makes several interesting points about the specificity of this historical world. He notes that *L'Argent* was made in 1982, after the election of Mitterrand in 1981 and his immediate launching of several radical socialist reforms, all of which failed, largely because of massive push-back from banks and corporations. Much that had been nationalized had to be privatized again, and many other reforms were reversed. So, the film was made in an atmosphere of great disappointment and a sense of crisis for many French intellectuals and progressives. As Price puts it, "*L'Argent* is in many ways a Mitterrandist film, an urgent plea to stem the tide of capitalism, and it could not have been more timely" (187).

interest in the kind of mild pornography they can find at that time. It is also one of only two hints at anything sexual in the film. Bresson's point is not clear, but it may have something to do with one of those brief, telling, indirect references to the environing world for these boys, here a certain "refined" (hidden behind fine art) commodification of beauty and sexuality, the kind of thing announced in Manet's *Olympia* and her defiant look. In a capitalist world, posing or exchanging sex for money is no different than any other exchange, since exchange value is the only value. (The other sexuality reference seems to have the same point. At the back of the café where Yvon goes to set up his role in the robbery, there are clearly prostitutes lolling about, among the other commodities.)

The two boys get on their motorbikes and successfully exchange the bill at the shop, despite the woman owner's suspicion. When her husband returns, he sees immediately that the bill is counterfeit, calls her an idiot, and promises to pass the bill off himself rather than call the police and have them confiscate it.

Our growing revulsion at the smugness and thoughtlessness of Norbert's family is particularly acute in the case of his mother, especially our parting glance at her. At a later point in the film, Norbert has been caught (one of the shop owners recognized him and followed him to his school, reported him),[5] and he gets into all sorts of trouble. His father is furious and acts as if it is all just an extremely irritating interruption of his business day, and his mother later visits the photo shop to solve the problem in a way she has clearly come to expect always works. Her clothes, her walk, the way she carries herself, all exude entitlement and snobbery. She says to the woman shopkeeper, "Then it's all understood? About my son?" and the shopkeeper promises never to reveal the son's name. Then the mother comes to the point: "Let me make up for the trouble this ridiculous matter has caused," and she pulls out an envelope full of cash. The shop owner pretends to protest with a "no, no," but the mother says, "I insist." I think it is fair to say that there is something deeply offensive, deeply and immediately representative of her image of herself, in her expressions and actions, even in her blood-red fingernails, which Bresson focuses on (plate 3). We also see again the use of doors to create a context of significance; the shopkeeper takes the

5. This is a peculiar plot point. By going to Norbert's school and accusing him of passing off a counterfeit bill, she is confirming what she had denied under oath, that any exchange had passed between them and Yvon, the only way he could have gotten the bill in question. Presumably, there was no way for the police to learn of what went on in the school.

unusual step of formally opening the door for the mother, an act suffused with class consciousness.

The pivotal episode in the narrative begins when the shop owner and his assistant Lucien make good on his promise to pass the bill off to Yvon. We first learn about Yvon by what can be only partially seen of him. First, a beautiful shot, dense in color, of his red gloved hands (plate 4). (This highlighted red begins what seems a connection between Yvon's working-class status, the bright-red robes of the justices who condemn him, and the blood that results from the revenge he takes.)[6] There is a long delay in showing his face (what counts in this world is his labor not him), and he enters the photo shop unsuspectingly for a routine payment.

Yvon accepts the counterfeit bills, tries to use them in a café, and is told they are false and that the waiter will keep the bills and call the police. Yvon's hair-trigger, violent reaction, and his deep sensitivity to feeling disrespected or humiliated, quickly show us his defensiveness, his quick propensity to violence, and his lack of resources to deal with the accusations against him. We see again that Bressonian emphasis on hands (plate 5), again as if to suggest a disconnect between his conscious intentions and his almost autonomous body. (In *A Man Escaped*, Bresson rarely cuts from Fontaine's hands to his face, as is conventional in such efforts.)

Yvon is not convicted (the shop owners don't press charges out of fear that their role in passing the bills will eventually be discovered), but the arrest on his record means that Yvon loses his job, cannot find another, and grows desperate to care for his wife and small daughter. In effect this false charge ruins his life. We experience the same sort of contempt for the shop owners and Lucien as we did for Norbert's family as they smugly congratulate themselves after the court proceeding, even congratulating and rewarding Norbert for his sangfroid in the lie. It also appears that Yvon's lack of standing in the legal world, which we have seen is run by and for the world of upper-middle-class and middle-class citizens (he is warned by the judge not to make such accusations again at such upstanding people as the shop owners), has either developed or brought out a fierce sense of pride and a deep anger at his humiliation. He bluntly rejects his wife's, Elise's, entreaties to explain the mistake to his employer and ask for his job back. Yvon insists he will not beg like a dog. (We see several times that all that is left of any possible agency for Yvon is refusal, refusal to defend

6. The other color scheme in the film involves the blue and black colors of police, of prisons, and of those in the society who can either exercise a police-like authority, like Norbert and his family, or be subjected to it, like the prisoners.

himself in the photo shop, to ask for his job back, to defend himself in court, to accept Lucien's repentance, even in his suicide attempt, to live.)

This all ultimately leads to Yvon's descent into the Parisian criminal world, his role in a botched bank robbery, and his conviction to a three-year prison term. The emphasis on color to set a certain mood or tonality in the film continues in the court scene and the reference again to red, the color of blood (plate 6).

Elise visits Yvon in prison, but she is uncommunicative and sullen, unresponsive to Yvon's pleas to keep faith with her, promises that they will start over when he gets out and that he will work hard. We learn later that she cannot tell him that their little girl has died.

The prison world, where the enemies of "legal" money are warehoused, is mostly presented episodically. Bresson takes some pains to show that although there is no money in prison there is a robust exchange economy in bartered goods, even in church. (There is a final exchange in the film, a contrast with mere exchange. In the garden where the kindly widow lives, Yvon picks chestnuts and shares them with the widow, does not ask for anything in return. A gift economy, not exchange.) The "engine" driving everything in that world too is their version of money. The prison sequence is interrupted occasionally. We see Lucien's new life of crime on the outside, a scheme for stealing debit cards after having spied the user's code. We learn later that although Lucien spends lavishly on himself, he also gives a lot of money away and even repays the photo shop owners for the money he stole from them. (We learn this from another interruption of prison life, when we learn that the photo shop is going under and the owners receive a large check from Lucien, prompting, somewhat bizarrely, the owner to shed a tear.) Lucien's Robin Hood swagger is taken down a notch when the judge at his trial notes that for all his charity, he is wearing an expensive suit. It remains unclear whether Lucien's check to the shop owners and his charity is the result of remorse (which seems highly unlikely) or gratuitous, grandstanding benevolence, a display of power and influence as showy as his fancy suits (which seems much more likely). He seems to be in the film to serve as a contrast with Yvon. Nothing Lucien can do can undo the catastrophic harm Lucien's and the owners' lying has wrought, no matter what he cavalierly offers now. And Lucien is a cheat and a thief, most likely a career criminal who belongs in prison. Yvon is guilty, but the collapse of his involvement with the world and his subsequent despair were not of his doing, as Lucien's is.

We see mail being delivered to the prison (blue baskets and blue uniforms) to a group of women who open, read, and classify all the mail. We surmise that they are to keep criminal communication from the prisoners.

It is in reading a letter over the shoulder of one of the women that we learn that Yvon and Elise's daughter, Yvette, had died of diphtheria before Elise's last visit, when she couldn't bring herself to say anything. The letter reaches Yvon, and he is clearly in some despair, weeping into his pillow as his two clownish but sympathetic cellmates sneak a drink. We also learn that Elise has been returning Yvon's letters and finally learn that she has left him. Somehow, word has reached his fellow prisoners who mock him mercilessly at dinner until we see the latent anger and violence in Yvon erupt again. When the guards try to subdue him, he begins to strike one of them but restrains himself. But he is still charged with the assault and sentenced to solitary. (He has raised a large serving spoon as a weapon, and Bresson takes time to endow that object with a significance beyond its mere physical presence, as if a still life that embodies everything crashing down on Yvon [plate 7].) The disintegration of Yvon accelerates rapidly from this point on. He begins to hide the tranquilizing pills he is being given daily until he has enough to attempt suicide. (Suicide, as we have seen, is an ever more frequent theme in Bresson, and what is important about his treatment is that it is not treated psychologically. The world he presents is such that it fails to inspire any commitment to it, once something happens to break the hold of an everyday, thoughtless conformist absorption.) He attempts the suicide off camera; we only see a shot of an ambulance loading someone inside, and only learn it was Yvon from the conversations of his two cellmates. We see his return to the prison and his eventual release.

As noted, we have detected occasional flashes of anger in Yvon, but nothing out of the ordinary. For the most part, he remains the same inexpressive, sullen, and completely enigmatic character we saw from the beginning. (As if to signal the implications of Norbert's original crime in what Yvon has become, when he is released from prison, Yvon is dressed in the very same clothes, blazer, blue shirt, khaki pants, that Norbert wears.) So we are shocked when the first thing he does upon his release is to murder and rob the two hotel keepers who run the ironically named Hotel Moderne. We were given no indication that Yvon's despair and anger could take such a form, no hint that he had become a sociopath, convinced now that only money matters, not human life. In a typical ellipsis, we don't see anything of the murders themselves. He enters the hotel, and in the next scene we only see an indirect indication of the murder, the blood he is washing off his hands and the bloody clothes he needs to change, and afterward his rifling through the cash desk and leaving.

The final twenty-three minutes of the film back-shadow in their significance everything that comes before. The straightforward developments seem inspired by a Tolstoy-like sentiment—that the presence of something like absolute unselfish goodness can provoke one of those moments of grace, unpredictable and wholly contingent, which can occasion a conversion, a reconnection with humanity, perhaps a newfound faith, in someone who has lost all sense of anything mattering other than his rage and hatred of the world, as if he has told himself, "They have taught me that all that matters in this world is money; so be it." We will learn that this widow certainly is the most saintly of any character in Bresson's work, and it is true that after murdering her and her family, and one shot of what appears to be reflection, Yvon turns himself in. But what we need to ask is what such a scenario might mean in the world that Bresson has shown us, whether Bresson counts it as a credible response to that world, the world of *L'Argent*, whether something like such a moment of grace could be a genuine reintroduction into humanity or a more desperate escape from it, or even perhaps a deeper moment of despair, that Yvon comes to feel that even his murderous rage, even money, doesn't matter. Either the widow's forgiveness and her willingness to risk death by caring for Yvon, her facing him calmly and unresistingly as he raises the axe above her, reignites in Yvon some sense of the value of human life, or it convinces him of the futility and meaninglessness of his campaign to vent his vengeful rage, that his robberies and murder are as pointless as the other possibilities available in *L'Argent* world.

In the village outside the prison, after the murders, Yvon is standing and looking at a window display of children's toys—something that no doubt calls his late daughter to mind—and an older woman passes by him as she goes to make a withdrawal at a post office. She seems to be aware that Yvon is following her, but appears unconcerned, even as he follows her all the way home. There is even the slightest of hints that she is inviting him to follow her, perhaps even welcoming what she suspects will be her own sacrifice. After all, very quickly she knows he is the murderer and he knows that she knows, and yet she still invites him in, feeds him, exposes her family to him, even carries coffee in the morning to where he is sleeping. She certainly takes no pleasure in her devoted service to the household, and when asked what she expects for such service, says only that she expects nothing, not a reward in the afterlife, not love in return, not gratitude. Her home though also means a radically contrasting context of nature, natural beauty, fecundity, growth, life, and some intimation of harmony and peace, none of which we have seen before in the film (plates 8 and 9). After following her, he finally simply enters her kitchen and sits down, and she is again not visibly disturbed. The two murders have obviously been the talk of the village, and she makes clear immediately that she knows that Yvon is the murderer, and yet again is undisturbed by the fact, and he even confesses it to her easily and with extreme sociopathic indifference.

This conversation with the woman seems to be the only self-conscious moment in the film, the only time Yvon tries to reflect or to understand himself, and his self-awareness is minimal to the point of absurdity.[7] This raises the question of his moral status in the film and the point of presenting him in this way. But we need to see more of this last quarter of the cinematograph.

We learn that she is a widow, that she lives with her father, two sisters, brother-in-law, and handicapped grandson, that after her husband died, her father fell apart, began to drink heavily, lost his piano pupils, and became abusive, a different person. She is also far and away the kindest person in all of Bresson's films, full of generosity and forgiveness, if also reckless in her disregard for her own and her family's safety. We see her slapped by her father when she brings Yvon coffee, and we see a great deal more of the natural environment of her home, as Yvon helps her with her chores, digging potatoes, hanging laundry.

As noted earlier, Yvon tells her later she does everything for the family and no one seems to even acknowledge it. "You do all the work yourself. You slave away for them. Why not just throw yourself in the river? Do you expect a miracle?" She answers simply, "I expect nothing." She bears the burden of such indifference, abuse, and ingratitude with the same stoic fortitude as Balthazar, and she must be constantly entertaining the thought that this remorseless sociopath will kill her and her family too. Bresson continues to use the camera to isolate and concentrate unusual attention on everyday objects, giving them an aura of significance and thus a nondiscursive intelligibility that again demonstrates the immediate if also unarticulated nature of that original significance. He is making here through the style of the photography alone an ontological point about the mode of being of the everyday that is as radical a philosophical point as the early Heidegger's.

The objects are photographed in a way that suggests they are not mere things; they are imbued with human significance; it is the way Bresson shows us that objects in a human world transcend their mere objectness, that their significance, meaningfulness in a human world is "real" not a matter of subjective projection and imposition. We might say that our hope is also aroused by the sudden and concentrated emphasis on one aspect of that meaningfulness, beauty, living natural beauty and the strange beauty of the interiors of the widow's home in this last segment. The interiors have the auratic presence of Chardin still lifes, and the natural scenes in summer seem to be bursting with life and fecundity. These all suggest a humanized

7. See the remarks by Amiel (1983), concluding rightly with "Tout est présence."

world of vibrant meaningfulness, a resonance that counters the sense of homelessness that dominates the film and inspires the hope that what Yvon has so clearly lost—a fundamental attachment to life itself—might be restored (not a reason to live but an experience of beauty that, as Keats noted, could itself help "bind us to the earth"). Even the murders, elliptically filmed again, are beautifully shot (plates 10, 11, and 12).

Even the father, who seems to rule over the house like a detached, angry god, given to alcoholic rages and even violence, is included in that the auratic sense of homeliness and harmony in the "look" of the house touches him too. Bresson is clearly not afraid to set these scenes of a potentially "binding" and redemptive beauty alongside the most fatalistic and brutally hopeless of situations. It is another example of his refusal of "ideology" of all kinds, as he once noted. We see and hear the father playing a beautiful Bach piece, with feeling and taste, even as we are reminded that his presence in the house is suffused with his alcohol problem, as we see him "through" the wine glass that must constantly accompany him throughout the day (plate 13).

The glass falls and breaks; the father keeps playing and the widow wordlessly cleans up the mess, as she is obviously used to doing.

Any hope inspired by the beauty of the household or the playing is forlorn, however, as we soon see in low light the results of the murderous rampage, tied together by the frantic dog rushing to and fro. We only see one direct scene of the killing, between Yvon and the widow, and this is all we see (plate 14). Afterward we see a pensive Yvon, but typically for Bresson, there is no articulation or even indication of his state of mind.

Since there is no expression of remorse or conscience, no explanation to the police, we have only that one reflective moment by Yvon after he tosses the axe into the water to resolve one of two possible interpretations of what he does, and it doesn't help much, if at all. Since Bresson preserves a bit of the murder scene from Tolstoy's story, the face-to-face encounter between the widow and Yvon, it is possible that her passivity, forgiveness, and essential goodness has moved Yvon to repent and reenter the human world. It is also true that we might recall that, back in prison, when Yvon had refused to join Lucien's failed escape attempt, his cellmate tells him that he has gotten his revenge on Lucien without doing anything and that "someone fond of you protects you from afar," and so we might think all of this violence had to occur to bring Yvon to some point of redemption, with the widow's blood sacrifice as the final event. But it is hard to find the remark about "protection" credible, given that Yvon has lost his job, his wife, his daughter, and his liberty, and that whoever was "protecting" him has made it possible for a mass murderer to kill many people. And since Bresson has subtracted all the dialogue by the woman and the penitent reflections of the murderer from the Tolstoy story, it is just as possible that Yvon has entered an even deeper level of despair, realizes that he can't keep slaughtering people for small amounts of money and simply "gives up" in more than a legal sense, no longer cares what happens to him, no longer cares at all. The unusual staging of the final scene, with the bar patrons still looking into the bar, not following Yvon into the police van, seems to suggest that theirs is our position, hopefully expecting that there will be something coming that will resolve the ambiguity, fix a meaning to what happened, and on our part that we will find a cinematic meaning in the event being filmed as it is (plate 15).

Neither of course is forthcoming.

Concluding Remarks

> Poetry, creative literature, is nothing but the elementary emergence into words, the becoming-uncovered, of existence as being-in-the-world. For the others who before it were blind, the world first becomes visible by what is thus spoken.[1]
>
> In "poetical" discourse, the communication of the existential possibilities of one's state-of-mind can become an aim in itself, and this amounts to a disclosing of existence.[2]

The claim has been that the numerous stylistic innovations in Bresson's films and his avoidance of the usual theatrical techniques prominent in commercial cinema raise the question of the point of the innovations. Why are the films so formally different from Hollywood movies? The argument was that, while the avoidance of filmed theater and the desire to make use of the medium-specific capacities of film and sound recording are certainly relevant, these innovations are best understood as implying varying philosophical commitments, where that most often means a commitment to a specific set of questions, paradoxes, puzzles, and ambiguities more than positions or theses, a kind of implied suggestion to look at the life we have created for ourselves *this* way, creating *these* crises and questions. The major commitments are not untypical of mid-twentieth-century thought, literature (Beckett, Pinter, Stevens, Larkin), and film (Antonioni, Bergman, Godard), but are in their details and tone uniquely Bressonian.

1. Heidegger (1988), 171–72.
2. Heidegger (2008), 205.

I have tried to identify as a major focus of Bresson's films the problem of meaningfulness, ranging from how things in our ordinary world make familiar sense to us in emerging into salience, or receding into insignificance, all the way to a basic orienting direction to our lives, or an experience of the collapse of such basic mattering experienced by, for example, Delbende and to some extent by the priest in *Diary*, Michel's fantasies about his uniqueness and the collapse of such an illusion in *Pickpocket*, Marie in *Balthazar*, *Mouchette* in Mouchette, Elle in *Une femme douce*, Charles in *Devil*, and Yvon in *L'Argent*.

To some extent employing the conceptual foci of Heidegger, the idea is then that at both the individual and collective level, this all occurs in ways that inherit possibilities of significance or meaningfulness in a historical world, a horizon of possible significance at a time, and our own relationship to such a world of significances is not a cognitive or a reflective matter, not a set of beliefs, but something like an attunement, a prediscursive sensitivity to such mattering. In addition, human beings have some but overall very little control over what happens to matter to them; they are subject to worlds of possible mattering rather than subjects of it. We find things mattering, in various degrees. If the world is a prison, what matters is resistance, some way of rejecting it, and escape. Everything in the prison comes to "mean" something in the light of what matters. If life itself is experienced as a prison, the same applies. Persons can experience crises of mattering, which largely make up the subject matter of many of Bresson's films, and this is tied to what is or is not available in a world. It manifests itself in profound boredom, anxiety, melancholy, hopelessness, or what we call now depression, in some films to the point of suicide.

The converse question, the possible bearing of the films on philosophy itself is another sort of issue. Here the claim has been not only that Bresson's films should be understood as a form of philosophical thought, but that traditional philosophy is impoverished if it makes no use of such a resource. Since life is obviously lived first-personally, not as a spectator, but as an agent actively driving one's life forward as it seems to one, then we want to ask questions such as, what is it like to feel betrayed, abandoned, anxious, afraid of death, hopeless, despairing, jealous, ignored, in love, and when are these experiences untrustworthy, defensive, paranoid, projections? There are no observational or analytic stances that can have access to what such experiences are like. And we don't just want to recognize the depiction of such experiences as "what it's actually like," we want to understand the place of such experiences in a life, how significant they are, what one might infer from them, what it is to take them into account or respond to such experiences, what is negligible or unimportant about them. More generally, we want to understand what might contribute to something mattering or failing to matter, how a historical world can serve as a source of such mattering, what it is like to risk a commitment to others in such a world, how that might fail, how and why unhappiness can slip into suicidal despair. With great auteurs, one can see that the ambition goes well beyond a case study of a particular imagined character and that the director aspires to a kind of typicality and generality that far transcends any sort of fictionalized documentary. And contrary to views of Bresson as presenting the eternal and unavoidable sinfulness of human being, I have tried to suggest that he is considerably more sensitive to the Western historical world as the context within which these questions must be raised, the emerging consumerist, technology-driven world that is especially prominent in his later films. It is hard to imagine why philosophy would not want to make use of such a phenomenologically rich medium, at least when the director is philosophically astute.

Such a philosophical reappraisal of Bresson should supplement, and in some areas challenge, the critical concentration on purely formal stylistic matters, and attention to putative religious dimensions of Bresson's work. The claim is even that his work contributes to philosophical understanding in a way that philosophy, including Heidegger's philosophy, cannot. They provide something Heidegger wanted and tried to give but could not in his neologisms, etymologies, and innovative syntax. They provide what Heidegger called an "attestation" (*Bezeugung*) of the picture of human existence he wanted to convince us of, what the phenomenologists call, somewhat too empirically, evidence (*BT*, §54). These are dimensions of human existence that are shown, what various human experiences are like, first-personally, disclosed by Bresson's selection and focus and very compressed indications of psychological life, features that would otherwise remain hidden, usually unnoticed in the flow of ordinary life. The claim for the truth of what is shown appeals to a recognition, an acknowledgment, on the part of the viewer of what he or she has always already known, lived through but not as such. The films don't "confirm" any "theses" about world and existence, but they "point" to, attune us to, essential and important aspects otherwise unnoticed in critical moments of a human life that cannot but be acknowledged once disclosed.

Since films are a mode of nondiscursive sense making, something felt, a sense of being awakened, reoriented, it is true that, just as for Heidegger himself, how we should think of any *discursive* articulation (like this one) of what are claimed to be modalities of nondiscursive intelligibility seems immediately paradoxical. But this is so only if such articulation is understood as some sort of paraphrase of what is otherwise merely shown, as if a kind of translation or decoding. That is not the case. The hope is that one can in interpretation, call up, remind a reader of their experience of the film itself (or promise such an experience), all as a way of returning to the film and remembering and reexperiencing it more fully. If a film can illuminate something that would otherwise go unnoticed, the discursive formulation is also a way of pointing back to the film, fully accepting the merely provisional and inadequate nature of that attempt "to point" successfully. To assume otherwise is to make the mistake of paraphrase in trying to understand any art object

This all means that the modality of literary and cinematic thinking is *disclosive* in different medium-specific ways. Something fundamental about the world of the characters or the lyric voice is revealed, uncovered, something about a historical world that can never itself be an object of attention in a world because always already presupposed for that world. In our time, which Heidegger calls "destitute," what is revealed is the very meager possibilities of any meaningful orientation in the world at all. In our time, art cannot be like the art of the Greek temple, radiantly manifesting the distinctiveness of the Greek world and the meaning of Being (beauty) that it inherits, or like the romantic hopes for a reconciliation with a living nature. Our worldly theme is absence, the unavailability of any common source of meaningfulness that could inspire and sustain an engaged commitment to the possibilities available within the world we find ourselves in.[3] Hegel for the first time showed us that philosophy can be its own time comprehended in thought. Bresson has shown us that film can be our own time as it really is, captured and felt in moving pictures and recorded sound.

3. To let Bresson have the last word:

> I believe, and I may be wrong, that the arts are in a general decline, are on their last legs and will eventually die. Perhaps from too much freedom, perhaps thanks to the unprecedented exposure everyone has to everything in our moment. I believe that the cinema, radio, television are killing the arts, but I also believe that cinema, radio, and television can revive the arts as well, perhaps with a totally different form. Maybe the word "art" will no longer have the same meaning. There is, I think, some hope there. I believe in cinematography as an absolutely new art, which we may not even quite understand yet. I believe in a cinematographic muse. The painter Degas said, "The arts don't talk to one another, they dance together." I believe that cinematography is, or will soon be, a wholly autonomous art, one different from the way we have thought of it so far, as the synthesis of other arts. It's an art that is absolutely hermetic, absolutely autonomous.
>
> It is very possible that cinema, as opposed to cinematography, will continue to exist. There's no reason for cinema as entertainment to stop existing, but I believe firmly in a serious cinematographic art, which would not be an entertainment, which would be, on the contrary, a means of engaging things more profoundly, an in-depth study of things, of people, and perhaps a means of discovery. (Bresson 1986, 14–15)

Acknowledgments

An earlier version of chapter 4 has appeared in the journal *Liberties* 4, no. 1 (Autumn 2023). I am grateful to interlocutors at the various occasions where earlier versions of chapters were given as lectures, in Geneva, Lausanne, and New York City, and at Brown University and the University of Chicago, as well as to students in a seminar on Bresson in the spring quarter of 2023 at Chicago and to Kyle Wagner for his support and advice throughout the process. I am especially grateful to Jonathan Hourigan for his advice and comments on earlier drafts of several chapters.

References

Adorno, Theodor. 1983. *Prisms.* Translated by Samuel and Chierry Weber. MIT Press.

Affron, Mirella Jona. 1998. "Bresson and Pascal: Rhetorical Affinities." In Quandt 1998, 165–87.

Amiel, Vincent. 1983. "L'Argent. La Pensée du present." *Positif*, no. 269–70 (July–August): 100.

Andrews, Dudley. 1981. "Desperation and Meditation: Bresson's *Diary of a Country Priest.*" In *Modern European Filmmakers and the Art of Adaptation*, 20–37. Frederick Unger Publishing.

Arnaud, Phillippe. 1986. *Robert Bresson.* Cahiers du Cinéma.

Assayas, Olivier, et al. 1989. "Autour de Pickpocket." *Cahiers du Cinéma*, no. 416 (February): 26–32.

Ayfre, Amédée, et al. 1968. *The Films of Robert Bresson.* Praeger.

Ayfre, Amédée. 1998. "The Universe of Robert Bresson." In Quandt 1998, 41–56.

Baby, Yvonne. 1967. "Le Domaine de l'indicible." *Le Monde*, March 14.

Bazin, André. 1998. "*Le Journal d'un curé de campagne* and the Stylistics of Robert Bresson." In Quandt 1998, 27–40.

Bernanos, Georges. (1937) 2002. *The Diary of a Country Priest.* Translated by Pamela Morris. Da Capo Press.

Bernanos, Georges. (1937) 2006. *Mouchette.* Translated by J. C. Whitehouse. NYRB Books.

Bernanos, Georges. (1955) 2019. *Liberty: The Last Essays.* Translated by Joan and Barry Ulanov. Cluny Media.

Bresson, Robert. 1986. *Notes on the Cinematograph.* Translated by Jonathan Griffin. NYRB Books.

Bresson, Robert. 2013. *Bresson on Bresson: Interviews, 1943–1983.* Edited by Mylène Bresson. Translated by Anna Moschovakis. NYRB Books.

Browne, Nick. 1977. "Narrative Point of View: The Rhetoric of *Au hasard, Balthazar.*" *Film Quarterly* 31 (1): 19–31.

Browne, Nick. 1980. "Film Form/Voice-Over: Bresson's *Diary of a Country Priest.*" In Quant 1998, 215–22.

Burnett, Colin 2004. "Inside Bresson's *L'Argent*." Interview with Jonathan Hourigan. *Offscreen* 8 (8). https://offscreen.com/issues/view/volume_8_issue_8.

Burnett, Colin. 2017. *The Invention of Robert Bresson: The Auteur and His Market*. Indiana University Press.

Burnett, Colin. 2021. "Cinéaste du rythme: Robert Bresson." *Screen Studies*, July 2. DOI: 10.5040/9781350970687.002.

Burnett, Colin. 2023. "'Tu penses, je fuis.' Reflections on Robert Pippin's 'The Clarifying Obscurity of Robert Bresson.'" https://colinatthemovies.wordpress.com/2023/12/31/.

Cameron, Ian. 1969. *The Films of Robert Bresson*. Praeger.

Cardullo, Burt. 2009a. *The Films of Robert Bresson: A Casebook*. Anthem Press.

Cardullo, Bert. 2009b. "Introduction." In Cardullo 2009a, xi–xxvi.

Ciment, Michael. 1998. "I Seek Not Description but Vision: Robert Bresson on *L'Argent*." In Quandt 1998, 499–512.

Collet, Jean. 1960. "Pickpocket." *Téléciné* 88 (March–April). Fiche filmographique, no. 363.

Cunneen, Joseph. 2003. *Robert Bresson: A Spiritual Style in Film*. Continuum.

Curran, Beth Kathryn. 2006. *Touching God: The Novels of Georges Bernanos and the Films of Robert Bresson*. Peter Lang.

Doebler, Peter. 2006. "Going Beyond Cézanne: The Development of Robert Bresson's Film Style in Response to the Painting of Paul Cézanne." *Cinema* 43 (April–June): 1–18.

Durgnat, Raymond. 1998. "The Negative Vision of Robert Bresson." In Quandt 1998, 411–52.

Durgnat, Raymond. 1999. "Pickpocket." *Film Comment* 35 (3): 48–53.

Estève, Michel. 1978. "Bernanos et Bresson." *Archives Bernanos*, no. 7: 39–52.

Estève, Michel. 1983. *Robert Bresson. La Passion du cinématographe*. Éditions Albatros.

Fried, Michael. 1976. *Absorption and Theatricality: Painting and Beholder in the Age of Diderot*. University of Chicago Press.

Fried, Michael. 1992. *Courbet's Realism*. University of Chicago Press.

Fried, Michael. 1998. *Art and Objecthood*. University of Chicago Press.

Gianopolou, Zina. 2024. "Being Animal in Robert Bresson's *Au hasard, Balthazar*." *Senses of Cinema*. http://www.sensesofcinema.com/2024/film-and-the-nonhuman/being-animal-in-robert-bressons-au-hasard-balthazar/.

Godard, Jean-Luc, and Michel Delahaye. 1998. "The Question." In Quandt 1998, 453–83.

Haneke, Michael. 2010. "Terror and Utopia of Form: Robert Bresson's *Au hasard Balthazar*." In *A Companion to Michael Haneke*, edited by Ray Grundmann, 565–74. Wiley-Blackwell.

Hanlon, Lindley. 1986a. *Fragments: Bresson's Film Style*. Associated University Presses.

Hanlon, Lindley. 1986b. "Introduction." In Hanlon 1986a, 19–23.

Hanlon, Linley. 1998. "Sound as Symbol in Mouchette." In Quandt 1998, 307–23.

Hayward, Susan. 1986. "Cohesive Relations and Texture in Bresson's Film 'L'Argent.'" *Substance* 16 (51): 52–68.

Heidegger, Martin. 1988. *The Basic Problems of Phenomenology*. Translated by Albert Hofstadter. Indiana University Press.

Heidegger, Martin. 2000. *Introduction to Metaphysics*. Translated by Gregory Fried and Richard Polt. Yale University Press. GA, Bd. 40.

Heidegger, Martin. 2008. *Being and Time*. Translated by John Macquarrie and Edward Robinson. HarperCollins.

Hourigan, Jonathan. n.d. "Interview with Tim Cawkwell, Parts I and II." Mastersofcinema.com at www.Robert-Bresson.com.

Indiana, Gary. 2014. "Pickpocket: Robert Bresson; Hidden in Plain Sight." https://www.criterion.com/current/posts/400-pickpocket-robert-bresson-hidden-in-plain-sight. Originally appeared in the Criterion Collection's 2005 DVD edition of *Pickpocket*.

Jacob, Gilles. 1967. "Mouchette: Une étude du film de Robert Bresson." *Cinema* 116:50–59.

Jones, Kent. 1998. "A Stranger's Posture: Notes on Bresson's Late Films." In Quandt 1998, 393–401.

Jones, Kent. 1999. *L'Argent*. BFI Publishing.

Jones, Kent. (1999) 2009. "Robert Bresson." In Cardullo 2009a, 1–3.

Kline, T. Jefferson. 1998. "Picking Dostoyevsky's Pocket: Bresson's Sl(e)ight of Screen." In Quandt 1998, 234–75.

Le Fanu, Mark. 1984. "Bresson, Tarkovsky and Contemporary Pessimism." *Cambridge Quarterly* 14 (1): 51–59.

Lopate, Phillip. 1999. "Mouchette." *Film Comment* 35 (3): 55–58.

McNeese, Lucy Stone. 1991. "'Miracle of the Flesh': Mouchette." *The French Review* 65 (2): 267–79.

Michelson, Annette. 1968. "Etc." *Commonweal*, November 29.

Millar, Daniel. 1969. "Pickpocket." In Cameron 1969, 82–89.

Morales, Alfonso Hoyos. 2023. "La Dialéctica Realidad/Verdad en las Notas sobre el cinematógrafo de Robert Bresson." *Thémata, Revista de Filosofia*, no. 68: 292–324.

Morari, Codruta. 2017. *The Bressonians: French Cinema and the Culture of Authorship*. Bergham.

Moravia, Alberto. 1998. "L'Argent." In Quandt 1998, 407–11.

Oudart, Jean-Pierre. 1977. "Modernité de Robert Bresson." *Cahiers du Cinéma* 273–83 (279–90): 27–30.

Petrie, Graham. 1968. "Mouchette by Robert Bresson." *Film Quarterly* 22 (1): 52–56.

Pipolo, Tony. 2010. *Robert Bresson: A Passion for Film*. Oxford University Press.

Pippin, Robert. 2010. *Hollywood Westerns and American Myth: The Importance of Howard Hawks and John Ford for Political Philosophy*. Yale University Press.

Pippin, Robert. 2017. *The Philosophical Hitchcock*. University of Chicago Press.

Pippin, Robert. 2020a. *Filmed Thought: Cinema as Reflective Form*. University of Chicago Press.

Pippin, Robert. 2020b. "Psychology Degree Zero: The Representation of Action in the Films of the Dardenne Brothers." In Pippin 2020a, 231–56.

Pippin, Robert. 2021a. "Authenticity in Painting: Remarks on Michael Fried's Art History." In Pippin 2021c, 102–24.

Pippin, Robert. 2021b. *Douglas Sirk: Filmmaker and Philosopher*. Bloomsbury.

Pippin, Robert. 2021c. *Philosophy by Other Means: The Arts in Philosophy and Philosophy in the Arts*. University of Chicago Press.

Pippin, Robert. 2023. "The Clarifying Obscurity of Robert Bresson." *Liberties* 4 (1): 74–103.

Pippin, Robert. 2024. *The Culmination: Heidegger, German Idealism, and the Fate of Philosophy*. University of Chicago Press.

Prédal, René. 1998. "Robert Bresson: L'Aventure intérieure." In Quandt 1998, 73–116.

Price, Brian. 2002a. "The End of Transcendence, the Mourning of Crime: Bresson's Hands." *Studies in French Cinema* 2 (3): 127–34.

Price, Brian. 2002b. "Une Femme Douce and the Spectrum of Revolt: Bresson's Transition to Color in the aftermath of May '68." *Framework* 43 (1): 127–60.

Price, Brian. 2007. "Sontag, Bresson, and the Unfixable." *Post Script: Essays in Film and the Humanities* 26 (2): 81–90.

Price, Brian. 2011. *Neither God nor Master: Robert Bresson and Radical Politics*. University of Minnesota Press.

Provoyeur, Jean-Louis. 2003. *Le cinéma de Robert Bresson. De l'effet de réel à l'effet de sublime*. L'Harmattan.

Quandt, James, ed. 1998. *Robert Bresson*. Cinematheque Ontario Monographs.

Quandt, James. 2009. "On Au hasard, Balthazar." In Cardullo 2009a, 81–86.

Rafferty, Terence. 2004. "The Austerity Campaign That Never Ended." *New York Times*, July 4. https://www.nytimes.com/2004/07/04/movies/film-dvd-the-austerity-campaign-that-never-ended.html?login=smartlock&auth=login-smartlock.

Rancière, Jacques. 2014. *The Intervals of Cinema*. Translated by John Howe. Verso.

Reader, Keith. 2000. *Robert Bresson*. Manchester University Press.

Renard-Georges, P. 1968. "Bernanos et Bresson." *Études bernanosiennes* 9.

Rosenbaum, Jonathan. 1998. "The Last Filmmaker: A Local, Interim Report." In Quandt 1998, 17–26.

Rushton, Richard. 2010. *The Reality of Film: Theories of Filmic Reality*. Manchester University Press.

Schrader, Paul. 1998. "Robert Bresson, Possibly." In Quandt 1998, 485–97.

Schrader, Paul. 2018. *Transcendental Style in Film: Ozu, Bresson, Dryer*. University of California Press.

Semoulé, Jean. 1993. *Bresson*. Flammarion.

Sitney, P. Adams. 1998. "Cinematography vs. the Cinema: Bresson's Figures." In Quandt 1998, 145–64.

Sloan, Jane. 1983. *Robert Bresson: A Guide to References and Sources*. G. K. Hall and Company.

Sontag, Susan. 1966. "Film and Theatre." *The Tulane Drama Review* 11 (1): 24.

Sontag, Susan. 1998. "Spiritual Style in the Films of Robert Bresson." In Quandt 1998, 57–72.

Thomson, David. (1987) 2009a. "Bresson and Lumière." In Cardullo 2009a, 193–98.

Thomson, David. 2009b. "The Earrings of Robert Bresson." In Cardullo 2009a, 199–202.

Trilling, Lionel. 1951. "W. D. Howells and the Roots of Modern Taste." *Partisan Review* 18 (September–October): 516–36.

Yacavone, Daniel. 2014. *Film Worlds: A Philosophical Aesthetics of Cinema*. Columbia University Press.

Index